Ludwig IV
Grand Duke of Hesse and by Rhine

Gebhard Zernin's Festschrift
to celebrate the unveiling
of the equestrian statue
in Darmstadt – 1898

Ludwig IV
Grand Duke of Hesse and by Rhine

Gebhard Zernin's Festschrift
to celebrate the unveiling
of the equestrian statue
in Darmstadt – 1898

Translated, edited and annotated by
Petra H. Kleinpenning

Bibliografische Information der Deutschen Nationalbibliothek: Die Deutsche Nationalbibliothek verzeichnet diese Publikation in der Deutschen Nationalbibliografie; detaillierte bibliografische Daten sind im Internet über dnb.dnb.de abrufbar.

Umschlagbild:
© Großherzogliches Familienarchiv im Staatsarchiv Darmstadt, D 27 A Nr. 48/272.

© 2023 Petra H. Kleinpenning
Herstellung und Verlag: BoD – Books on Demand, Norderstedt

ISBN: 978-3-7431-5372-1

All rights reserved. No part of this book may be reproduced, stored in a retrieval system, or transmitted, in any form or by any means, electronic, mechanical, photocopying, recording, or otherwise, without the prior written consent of the copyright holder.

Contents

	Page
Acknowledgement	7
Introduction	13
Notes to the reader	16
Zernin's Festschrift	17
Foreword	19
Birth and baptism (1837); childhood and education (1838–1853)	20
Confirmation and entry into the Hessian military service (1854)	25
Studies at the Universities of Göttingen and Giessen (1856–1857)	31
Entry into the Prussian military service (1859)	35
Engagement (1860) and marriage (1862)	42
Activity in the Hessian military service (1862–1866)	45
Participation in the Campaign of the Main (1866)	46
Participation in the Franco-German War (1870–1871)	49
Leadership of the Grand-ducal Hessian Division (1870–1877)	54
Sovereign (1877–1892)	57
Last illness and death (1892)	64
Character sketch and conclusion	66
The unveiling of the equestrian statue in Darmstadt (1898)	77
Conclusion	96
Bibliography	99
Index	103

Acknowledgement

I gratefully acknowledge the permission of the Hessian State Archive Darmstadt to include in this publication two photographs from the Grand Ducal Family Archive at the State Archive Darmstadt as well as two further pictures from the State Archive's collection, with accession numbers D 27 A Nr. 48/272, D 27 A Nr. 48/280, R 4 Nr. 25425, and R 4 Nr. 30947 respectively.

Petra H. Kleinpenning

Partial family tree of Grand Duke Ludwig II of Hesse

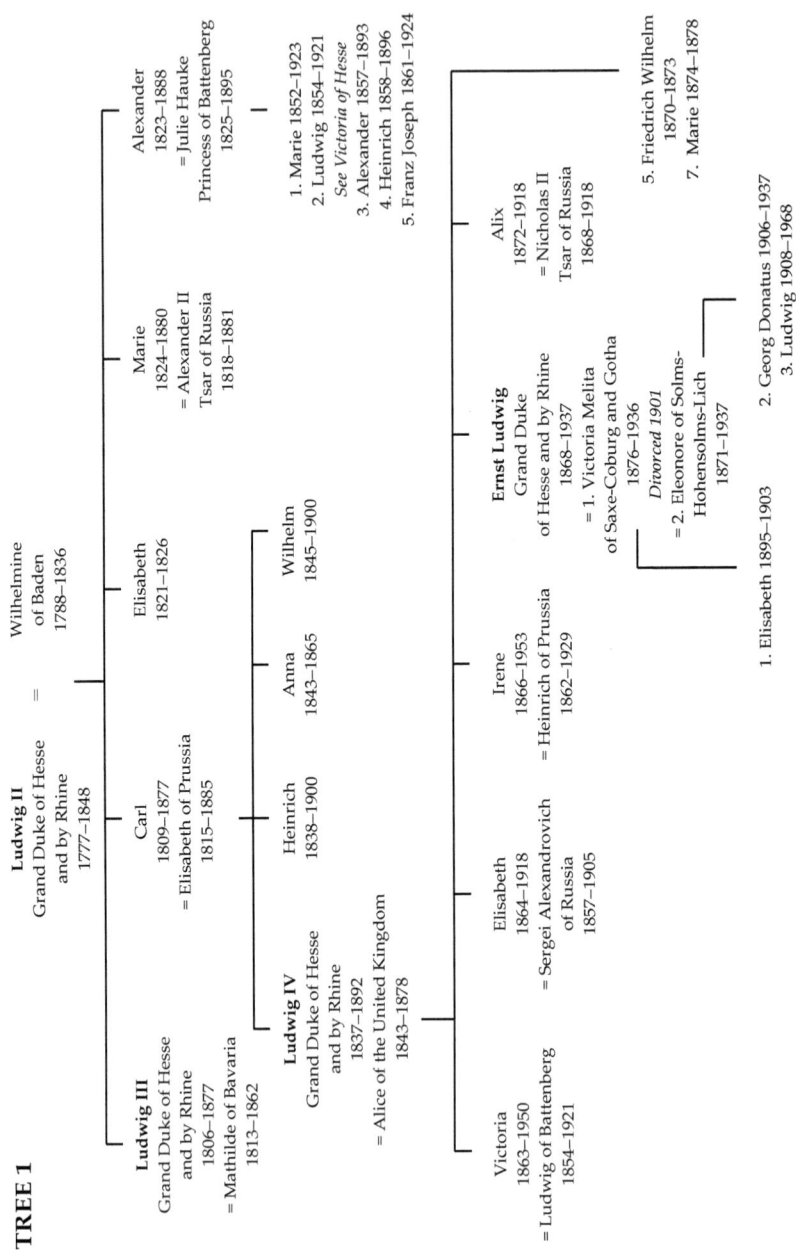

TREE 1

Partial family tree of King Friedrich Wilhelm II of Prussia

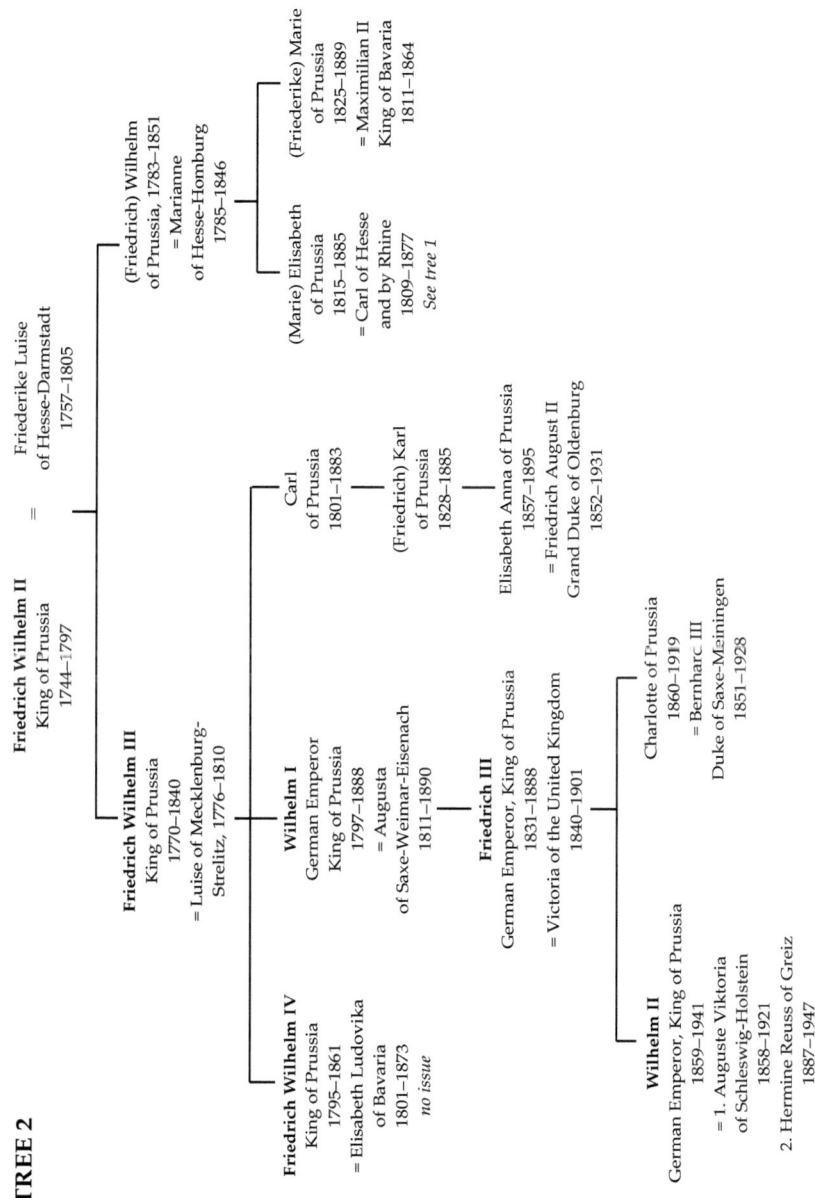

TREE 2

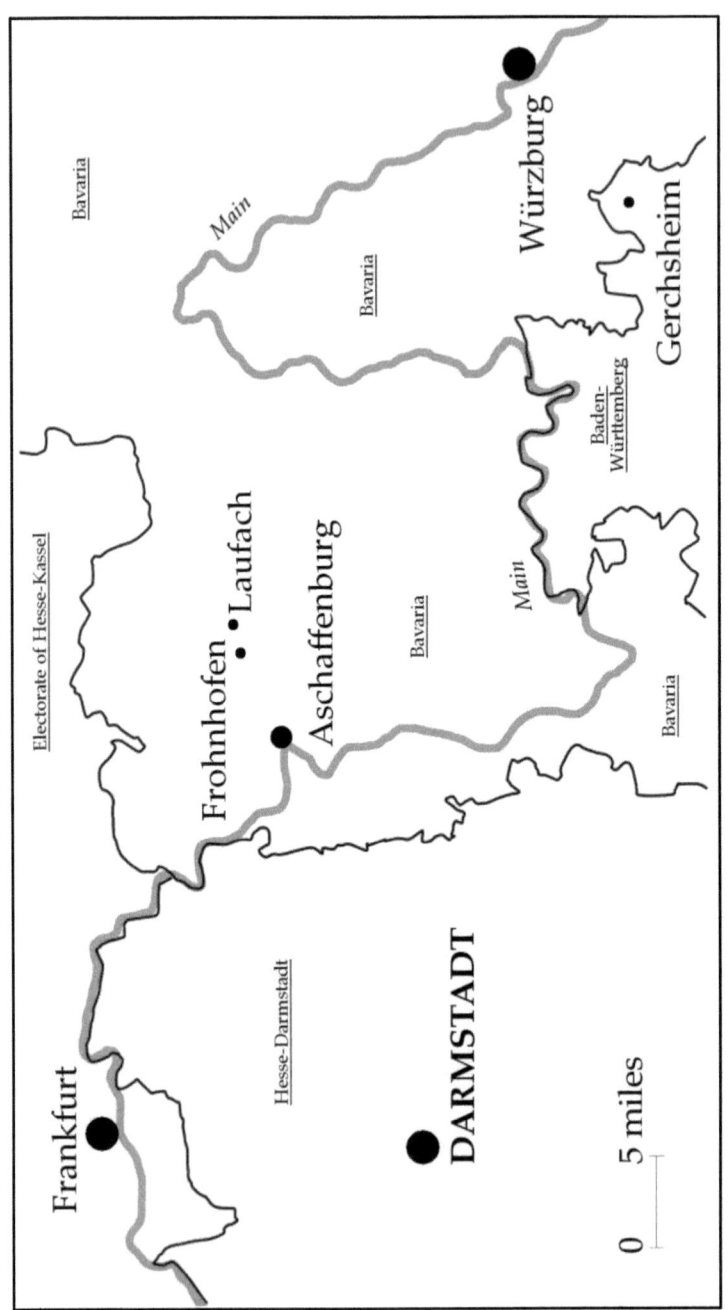

Locations of battles along the River Main in July 1866

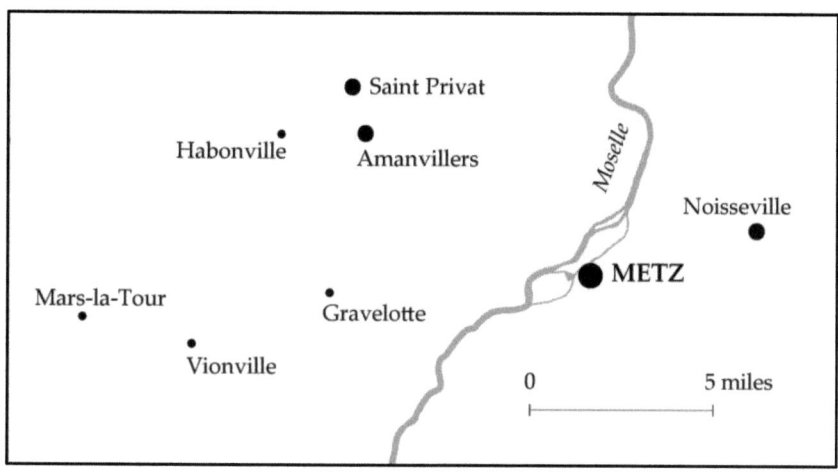

Locations of battles near Metz in France in August-October 1870

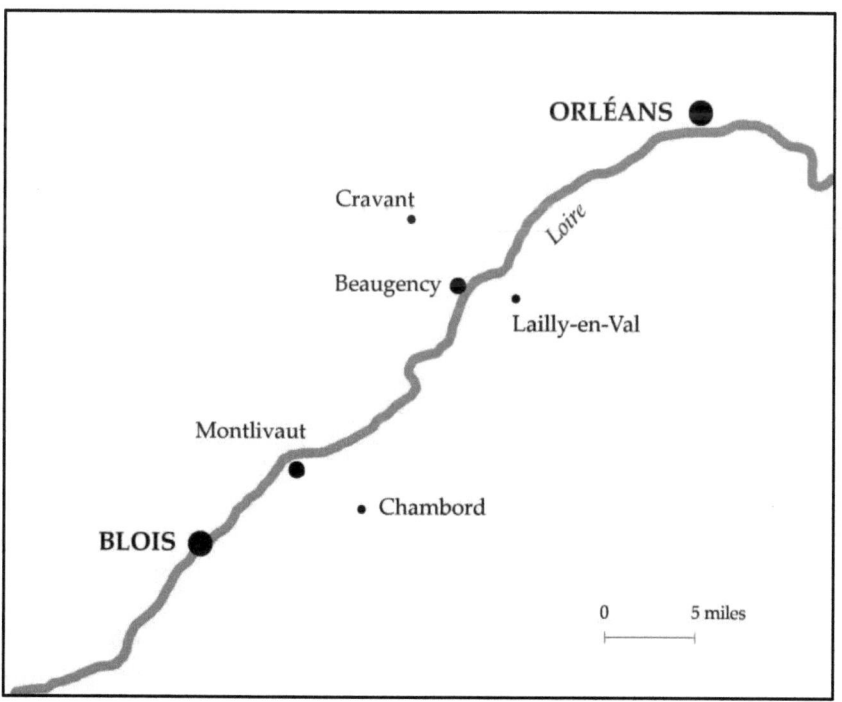

Locations of battles along the River Loire in France in December 1870

Introduction

Grand Duke Ludwig IV of Hesse and by Rhine (1837–1892) was born and died in the city of Darmstadt, Germany. While the domestic situation of the Grand Duchy of Hesse and by Rhine (or Hesse-Darmstadt) was relatively peaceful during Ludwig's lifetime, Hesse was swept up in the process of unification of German-speaking states into the German Empire. This process was not without its struggles. Two wars were fought before the German Empire was established: the Austro-Prussian War of 1866 and the Franco-Prussian War of 1870–1871. Ludwig lived through and actively participated in both these wars before he came to the throne of the Grand Duchy of Hesse and by Rhine in 1877.

Not much has been written about the life of Grand Duke Ludwig IV. There is no complete biography of Ludwig IV thus far. The literature available on him deals primarily with his military career. However, information regarding Ludwig as a private person and summary information regarding his political views can be found in letters, memoirs, and biographies of his wife, children and other relatives. Of particular interest are the letters from his wife, Princess Alice, to her mother, Queen Victoria, in which the princess also described her deep concerns regarding her husband's safety during the weeks when he was away during the wars of 1866 and 1870–1871.[1] Ludwig's son and successor, Ernst Ludwig, wrote memoirs later in his life, which included a chapter focusing on his parents.[2] From these letters and memoirs, from the

---

[1] Alice Grand Duchess of Hesse, *Alice, Grand Duchess of Hesse, Princess of Great Britain and Ireland: Biographical Sketch and Letters* (New York: G. P. Putnam's Sons, 1885).

[2] Ernst Ludwig Grossherzog von Hessen und bei Rhein, Eckhart G. Franz, and Golo Mann, *Erinnertes: Aufzeichnungen des letzten Grossherzogs Ernst Ludwig von Hessen und bei Rhein* (Darmstadt: E. Roether, 1983), 44–56.

memoirs of Ludwig's first daughter, Victoria,[3] as well as from the memoirs of his youngest surviving daughter, Alix – in Sophie Buxhoeveden's biography[4] – Ludwig emerges as a humble and kind-hearted man and soldier in heart and soul, who was anything but war-hungry.

Soon after the death of Grand Duke Ludwig IV on 13 March 1892, there were calls to erect a monument dedicated to him in Darmstadt, the capital of the Grand Duchy. A monument committee was established, which was chaired by Bruno, Prince of Ysenburg and Büdingen (1837–1906).[5] As Grand Duke Ludwig IV had been a soldier in heart and soul, it was only natural that this monument would portray him as such, and the choice of an equestrian statue was made. The statue was unveiled on 25 November 1898, which also happened to be the birthday of his son and successor, Grand Duke Ernst Ludwig, as well as that of Ernst Ludwig's wife, Grand Duchess Victoria Melita.

Gebhard Zernin (1830–1914) was asked to write a biographical sketch of Ludwig IV on the occasion of the unveiling of the equestrian statue. Gebhard Zernin, also known as Eduard Zernin, was promoted to lieutenant general (*Oberstleutnant*) à la suite of the Infantry in 1871, and to captain (*Hauptmann*) à la suite in Darmstadt in 1876. He was also a military writer as well as the chief editor and publisher of the *Allgemeine Militär-Zeitung*, a military weekly magazine. Thus he was ideally suited to the task of writing such a biographical sketch. His sketch, entitled *Ein*

---

[3] Victoria Marchioness of Milford Haven. *Recollections: The Memoirs of Victoria Marchioness of Milford Haven, 1863–1914*. Typescript of the recollections. Broadlands archives. MS62/MB/21. University of Southampton Special Collections (Southampton, UK, n.d.).

[4] Sophie Buxhoeveden, *The Life and Tragedy of Alexandra Feodorovna, Empress of Russia: A Biography* (London: Longmans, Green, 1930).

[5] *Darmstädter Zeitung*, 26 November 1898, morning edition.

Lebensbild von Ludwig IV. Grossherzog von Hessen und bei Rhein. Festschrift zur Feier der Enthüllung des Reiterdenkmals zu Darmstadt, was published by Großherzoglicher Staatsverlag in Darmstadt.

As expected of a commemorative publication, the sketch speaks only well of Grand Duke Ludwig IV and of Hesse, in wordings that modern non-German readers may perceive as rather patriotic. Like other publications on Grand Duke Ludwig IV, Zernin's *Festschrift* is not a full biography either and focuses on the military aspects of Ludwig IV's life, containing details of the wars in which Ludwig fought as well as anecdotes and memories of Ludwig contributed by fellow soldiers. Grand Duke Ludwig IV's reign, his style of rule, and his political views are discussed only summarily. However, the details provided regarding his childhood, parental family, education and military career in Hesse and Prussia make it a publication that will be valuable to a wider public readership than those interested merely in military affairs.

Zernin's *Festschrift*, written and published on the occasion of the unveiling of the equestrian statue, was printed in Fraktur and was, until now, only available in German. The present publication includes the first English translation of the full text of this commemorative biographical sketch. This translation is followed by an account of the unveiling ceremony based on its coverage in the local newspaper – *Darmstädter Zeitung*.

Petra H. Kleinpenning
Translator, editor, and annotator

March 2023

Notes to the reader

Zernin included quotations from letters, journals, and memoirs of Grand Duke Ludwig IV's wife, Princess Alice, and of Queen Victoria and Prince Consort Albert. He used published German translations for this purpose. In the present translation of Zernin's *Festschrift*, these quotations are taken from the original authorised English publications and the bibliographical references in the relevant footnotes have been adjusted accordingly.

The notes in the original German text of Zernin's *Festschrift* have been included and are presented here as footnotes. Supplementary explanatory information to Zernin's *Festschrift* provided by the editor is also included in footnotes. In order to distinguish between the two types of footnotes, those taken from the original *Festschrift* are labelled as 'Notes by G. Zernin'.

Zernin's *Festschrift* included neither an index nor a bibliography. An index and a concise bibliography have been added to the translation of the *Festschrift*, together with family trees and a few maps to provide non-German readers a better understanding of the family ties and the geography of the places mentioned in the *Festschrift*.

Petra H. Kleinpenning

Zernin's Festschrift

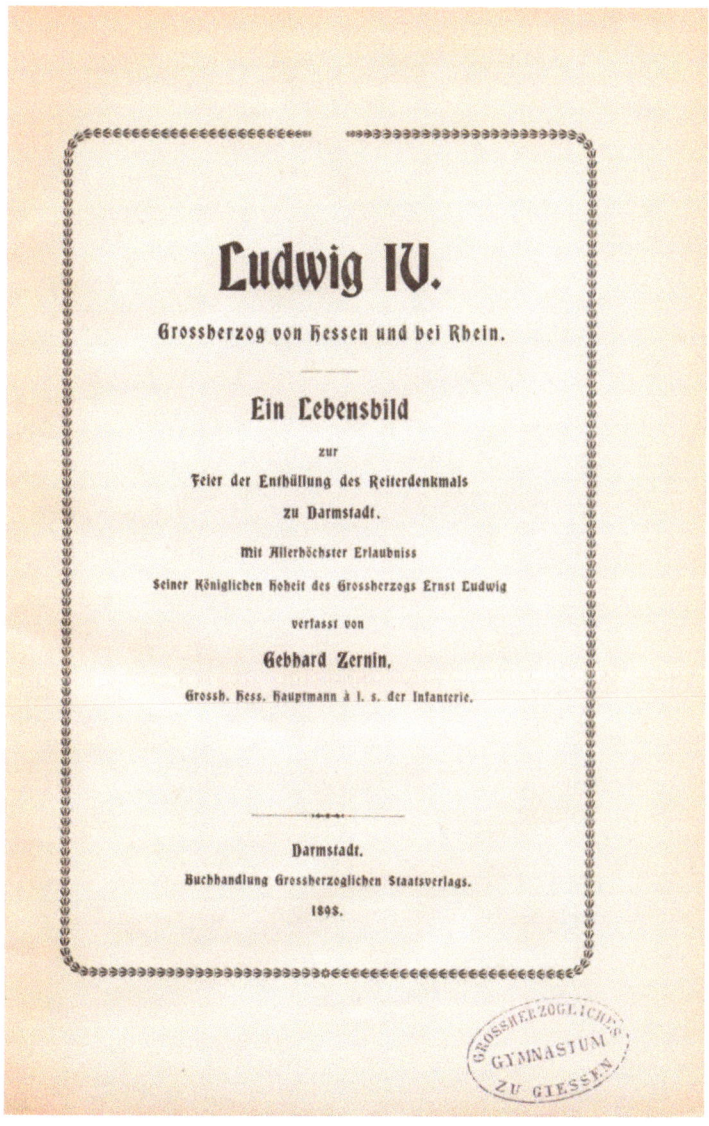

The title page of the original publication of
Gebhard Zernin's *Festschrift* on Grand Duke Ludwig IV

Photo of Grand Duke Ludwig IV included in the original publication of Gebhard Zernin's *Festschrift*

Foreword

The purpose of this text is to provide both the Hessian citizen and the soldier a concise but reliable picture of the life of Grand Duke Ludwig IV of Hesse and by Rhine on the occasion of the unveiling of his statue on the birthdays of the current Grand Duke and his consort on 25 November 1898. Such a summarizing portrait was not yet available; however, the leader of the Grand-ducal Hessian (25th) Division during the glorious Franco-German War of 1870–1871 made the most justified claims to a biography that puts his merits in the brightest light. In the following pages, an attempt is made to draw up a short character sketch, for which the rich treasures of the Grand-ducal House and State Archives, as well as the existing rich literature have been consulted.

The author wishes to express his most sincere gratitude to those gentlemen who supported him in the elaboration of this biographical sketch with advice and assistance, particularly to the gentlemen of the Grand-Ducal General-Adjutancy and the Director of the Grand-Ducal Court and State Archives, as well as numerous other individuals.

May this short piece of writing contribute to keep alive the memory of the benevolent sovereign, the gallant commander, the brave soldier, and good man whose features have been embodied by Professor Schaper's[6] master hand and will welcome every visitor with a serious but friendly look from the pedestal of his equestrian statue on Darmstadt's Paradeplatz!

Gebhard Zernin

---

[6] Professor Friedrich ('Fritz') Schaper (1841–1919) was a sculptor and a member of the Royal Academy of the Arts of Berlin. He received a decoration as Commander 2nd Class of the Ludwig Order on 25 November 1898. (*Hessisches Regierungsblatt, Beilage 32*, 29 December 1898, 270)

Birth and baptism (1837); childhood and education (1838–1853)

On 12 September 1837, great joy reigned in the newly built palace of Prince Carl of Hesse and by Rhine on Wilhelminenstrasse in Darmstadt. At a quarter past nine in the evening, a Hessian prince saw the light of day as the firstborn of a very happy princely marriage. In his veins flowed both Hessian and Prussian blood. He was the first son of the aforementioned Prince Carl (1809–1877), the son of the then ruling Grand Duke Ludwig II of Hesse and by Rhine (1777–1848), and Princess Elisabeth (1815–1885), the daughter of Prince Wilhelm of Prussia (1783–1851) and a cousin of Emperor Wilhelm the Great. The young prince received holy baptism on 28 September 1837, whereby he was given the baptismal names Friedrich Wilhelm Ludwig Carl. His godparents were King Friedrich Wilhelm III of Prussia (1770–1840), Grand Duke Ludwig II of Hesse (1777–1848), Prince Wilhelm of Prussia (1783–1851), Princess Maria Anna of Prussia (1785–1846), née Princess of Hesse-Homburg, the ruling Landgrave Ludwig of Hesse-Homburg (1770–1839), and the Hereditary Grand Duke, subsequently Grand Duke Ludwig III of Hesse (1806–1877) who was the elder brother of Prince Carl. The baptismal names were taken from the first names of the individual godparents.

The baptizand was described by his contemporaries as a strong and physically well-formed boy who grew under the happiest conditions. He had just completed the first year of his life and made his first successful attempts at walking, when – on 28 November 1838 – arrived his little baby brother, who received the names Heinrich Ludwig Wilhelm Adalbert Waldemar Alexander in holy baptism on the day after Christmas Day of that year. It must be noted that both brothers held together loyally throughout their later lives and experienced many things together; they were not only brought up and educated together but were also simultaneously destined for military careers and entered military service on the same day. Subsequently, in the great struggle for German independence on French soil, both brothers acquired great fame during the war and returned to their homeland as excellent troop leaders. Both brothers also suffered the same bitter fate of having their wives snatched from them by death after a relatively short period of time.[7] Both princes always remained close in faithful brotherly love, even when they were far from one other – they remained best friends from cradle to grave!

A faithful childhood friend of Princess Carl of Hesse, the noble Duchess Helene of Mecklenburg (Orléans),[8] who had married the eldest son of King Louis Philippe I of France in 1837 and had also given birth to a son in 1838, expressed her congratulations on the arrival of the second prince in Darmstadt with the following significant words: *May the Lord bless our sons with his spirit and his strength, that they may one day become rather capable men and rise to our much demanding times; for less than ever now a man's high birth helps him to achieve something: it rather becomes another obligation for him to distinguish himself before others by gifts of the spirit and the heart. Noble thinking, goodness of heart, and extensive knowledge is the only dowry by which our children can enter their careers with the hope of becoming useful to their fellow human beings and fulfilling their duties before God. It has become a beautiful but difficult task for us to prepare them and to plant the seeds of their subsequent fruits in their tender minds. That is why I find the job of a mother so serious and so great.*

One explanation for why both princes were destined for military careers at the same time could be that, at the time, one could not imagine that Prince Ludwig of Hesse would one day ascend to the throne of the Grand Duchy. The situation was similar

---

[7] Grand Duchess Alice of Hesse and by Rhine died of diphtheria on 14 December 1878. Caroline Willich von Pöllnitz, the first morganatic wife of Prince Heinrich, died on 6 January 1879 after giving birth to a son, Karl.

[8] Duchess Helene of Orlèans, née Princess Helene Luise Elisabeth of Mecklenburg-Schwerin (1814–1858).

to that of the Prince of Prussia, who subsequently became king and was called Emperor Wilhelm I, who could by no means cherish the thought that he would succeed his brother Friedrich Wilhelm IV as King of Prussia and saw a military career as his future, until he became sovereign at the age of 64 after the death of the Prussian ruler in 1861.

We have received the following reports on the early childhood of the two Hessian princes: *In caring for her two sons, Princess Carl felt very happy and repeatedly expressed the wish and hope that this happiness would also be bestowed on her sister-in-law, the Hereditary Grand Duchess Mathilde.*[9] *She used any time not taken up by other duties to occupy herself with the children, and these were so attached to their mother that she sometimes had to tear herself away from them by force.*[10]

However, one must not assume that both princes were spoiled 'mama's boys'. On the contrary, their upbringing was very precisely regulated and occasionally rather strict. During the summer, the family of Prince Carl, who preferred a secluded life just as much as his wife did, lived at the grand-ducal country estate at Seeheim on the Bergstrasse (Mountain Road) or at the simple, but rather picturesque, country seat of the Prince on Rosenhöhe (Rose Hill) east of Darmstadt, which provides splendid views of the forest-crowned heights of the Odenwald mountain range. For variety's sake, they would stay for several weeks at the romantic Fischbach Castle in Silesia, a property that belonged to Princess Carl's parents. There, the imagination of her young sons was stimulated in a lively manner by the fairy tales of Rübezahl, the mountain spirit of the Giant Mountains, and his rule

---

[9] Hereditary Grand Duke Ludwig of Hesse, subsequently Grand Duke Ludwig III, had married Princess Mathilde Karoline of Bavaria (1813–1862) in 1833.

[10] [Note by G. Zernin:] Cf. Ferdinand Bender, *Elisabeth, Prinzessin Carl von Hessen und bei Rhein, geb. Prinzessin von Preußen: Ein Lebensbild* (Darmstadt: Waitz, 1886), 47.

in the mountain gorges. Princes Ludwig and Heinrich visited Fischbach Castle for the first time in the summer of 1842; they witnessed the solemn confirmation of their mother's younger sister, Princess Marie[11] – subsequently Queen-Mother of Bavaria, wife of King Maximilian II. The stay in Silesia was extended into the autumn and left the princes with the best impressions; it also had the most benevolent effects on their physical development.

The following year, Princess Carl gave birth to a daughter on 25 May 1843. The baby girl was baptized on 18 June, which happened to be her mother's birthday and the day of the Battle of Waterloo in 1815, and received the baptismal names Maria Anna Wilhelmine Elisabeth Mathilde. A third son, Prince Wilhelm Ludwig Friedrich Georg Emil Philipp Gustav Ferdinand, was born on 16 November 1845. All three princes and their only sister, Princess Anna, developed rather well physically and mentally; they grew up cheerfully and had a sunny childhood and youth.

The first tutor of the two oldest princes was a highly educated nobleman and officer of strong character: Adolf von Grolman.[12] The private lessons were entrusted to the most reliable individuals. Instruction in the main subjects was given by *Hofrat* Becker,[13] a teacher at the Ludwig-Georg-Gymnasium at the time (deceased as *Geheimer Oberschulrat*); religious instruction was provided by court preacher Dr Bender;[14] *Hofrat* Feder[15] was their

---

[11] Princess Marie of Prussia (1825–1889) made her Confirmation in the Evangelical Christian Church. While she was an Evangelical Christian, her future husband was a Roman Catholic. The evangelical procuration wedding ceremony took place in Berlin on 5 October 1842, and the catholic wedding ceremony in Munich on 12 October of that year. Marie converted to Catholicism on 12 October 1874, over 10 years after her husband's death.

[12] Adolf Wilhelm Theodor von Grolman (+1887), captain and tutor of Princes Ludwig and Heinrich from September 1845.

[13] Theodor Andreas Becker (?–1895).

[14] Dr Ferdinand Bender (1816–1902).

[15] Karl August Ludwig Feder (1790–1856), *Hofrat* and librarian at the court.

newer languages teacher. Other teachers were A. F. Herbold,[16] cadastral engineer Thomas,[17] and military widows' funds calculator Wiegand. Special attention was paid to physical exercises; the princes received their gymnastics training from the famous gymnastics teacher and *assessor* Edmund Spiess[18] and fencing lessons from fencing master Hahn, as well as instruction in riding, dancing, swimming, etc. The fine arts, which were always highly regarded at the Darmstadt court, were also not neglected: court painter Lucas[19] taught the princes how to draw, and Miss von Heldenberg taught them how to play the piano.

According to the above account, the princes appear to have received a good all-round education. Their education followed the guidelines used by the wise men of ancient times. The subsequent Grand Duke Ludwig IV always kept this in mind and, on 10 June 1888, even personally entered the motto *'Mens sana in corpore sano'* into the interesting autograph album *In Luft und Sonne – Zum Besten der Ferienkolonien Deutschlands* (page 38), published by Schorers Familienblatt in Berlin in 1888.

---

[16] Anton Friedrich Herbold, school vicar and teacher at the city boys' school in Darmstadt.

[17] Heinrich Ludwig Thomas (1810–1868), surveyor 1st class and cadastral draughtsman at the cadastre office.

[18] Zernin mentioned Edmund Spiess in the original German publication of his *Festschrift*. However, the famous gymnastics teacher may not have been Edmund Spiess but Adolf Spiess (1810–1858). Adolf Spiess was born in Lauterbach in the Vogelsbergkreis district of Hesse and worked in Basel from May 1844 to 1848. In 1848, he came to Darmstadt to introduce gymnastics into the schools in Hesse and to train gymnastics teachers. Moreover, he was appointed as *assessor* to superintend this work in September 1849.

[19] Presumably August Lucas (1803–1863). He was a graphic artist and landscape painter from Darmstadt who studied at the art academy in Munich. He moved to Italy in 1829, but returned to Darmstadt in 1834 and worked as a drawing instructor at two local schools from 1841 onwards.

Confirmation and entry into the Hessian military service (1854)

In Easter 1854, the two princes reached a significant stage of life at which they were allowed to join the ranks of the adult members of the Christian Church. Their confirmation was celebrated in the court church in Darmstadt on 11 April 1854, the Tuesday following Palm Sunday. Both Prince Ludwig and his younger brother Heinrich solemnly professed their Protestant faith in a loud voice. That very morning, the reigning Grand Duke of Hesse, Ludwig III, had appointed both princes as 'aggregated lieutenants' to the 1st Grand-ducal Hessian Infantry Regiment, now No. 115, and awarded them the Grand Cross of the Ludwig Order. It was an uplifting celebration. The entire court was assembled in the court church, the recently formed church choir under the direction of court music director C. A. Mangold[20] sang selected choral music *a capella*, and court preacher Bender made a moving speech. All the teachers of the two princes had received invitations to the church celebration.

On 17 April, a large parade took place on Paradeplatz in front of the Grand-ducal Residential Palace. Grand Duke Ludwig III attended the parade with Princes Carl, Georg, and Emil of Hesse. On this occasion, the two youngest Hessian officers were presented to the assembled officer corps by the minister of war, Baron von Schäffer-Bernstein[21] – almost at the same spot where the equestrian statue stands today – after this general had given a solemn address to the princes, which made a significant impression on their sensitive minds.

---

[20] Carl Amadeus (or Amand) Mangold (1813–1889), a musician, director, and composer who worked as musical director at the Hessian court theatre.
[21] Baron Friedrich Ferdinand von Schäffer-Bernstein (ca. 1790–1861), Grand-ducal Hessian General of the Infantry and minister of war.

Now the front service in the Grand-ducal Hessian Army Division, as it was called until 1866, began. Both the princes – the elder almost 17 and the younger almost 16 years old – were not spared in any way and were trained in all forms of practical military service; they had to go on guard duty like any other lieutenant, lead their platoons in battalion exercises, and undergo various branches of the company service under the guidance of a captain – in other words, they had to attempt to master what a lieutenant in the troops should do. On 9 June 1855 – on the birthday of the reigning Grand Duke Ludwig III – both princes were promoted to the rank of lieutenant general.

Meanwhile, the question of how best to arrange the academic training of the two princes was discussed in the leading circles of Darmstadt. Grand Duke Ludwig III had attended lectures at the University of Leipzig as the hereditary grand duke, before assuming his role in the government of Hesse; therefore, it was considered appropriate that Princes Ludwig and Heinrich would also attend a German university. The only remaining decision was on the best time for these studies in order to avoid them from coinciding with their military training and which university would be selected for this purpose. The matter was considered very conscientiously, and captain von Grolman turned to Colonel Fischer for advice,[22] with the latter then stationed at Coblenz, who had guided Prince Friedrich Wilhelm of Prussia,[23] the future Emperor Friedrich III, as governor at the University of Bonn in the fall of 1849. The following eight questions were submitted to Colonel Fischer:

1. How old was the prince when he went to university?
2. How far advanced was his academic training at the time?

---

[22] Friedrich Leopold Fischer (1789–1857) was a colonel (*Oberst*) in the Prussian army and military governor of Prince Friedrich Wilhelm from January 1849 onwards.

[23] Prince Friedrich Wilhelm of Prussia (1831–1888). He would marry Victoria, the Princess Royal, in 1858.

3. Were the lessons purely in military science?
4. Had he already practiced military service and how?
5. What public lectures did the prince attend, and in which disciplines were *privatissima* given to him? And in which order and by whom?
6. In what ways did the prince participate in university life?
7. Did the prince begin his practical military service immediately after his university career?
8. How was the prince acquainted with the practical civil service?

Colonel Fischer provided the following answers in a rather detailed letter:

His Royal Highness Prince Friedrich Wilhelm had just completed his eighteenth year when he went to the University of Bonn in the fall of 1849.

He had the knowledge of a 'Primaner', a student in one of the two highest grades of Prussian grammar school.

Lessons in military science were given only in tactics.

The prince had been trained as an infantryman with a rifle and marching as early as in his tenth year. In May 1849, at the age of 18, the prince served as a platoon leader in the 1st Foot Guard Regiment in Potsdam.

With regard to lectures in Bonn, the prince usually attended a public lecture and several privatissima *in each semester, for a total of together 18–20 hours per week. In the first semester the prince attended the following lessons: History of Roman law with Professor Walter weekly and a* privatissimum *as revision. History of the Middle Ages with Professor Löbell, at the same time as a style exercise. Repetitorium Roman classics with Professor Curtius.*[24] *French conversation and style with Professor Monnard.*

---

[24] Ernst Curtius (1814–1896) was an archaeologist and ancient historian. Grand Duke Ludwig IV was also interested in archaeology. His daughter Victoria

> *In the second semester, the prince attended the following classes: History of German law with Professor Perthes publicly and a* privatissimum *as revision. Roman law with Professor Walter and History of the sixteenth and seventeenth centuries with Professor Löbell as earlier. French conversation and style with Professor Monnard, and the same for English with Dr Walter and Perry.*
>
> *(The prince made a journey through the Alps, a part of Upper Italy and southern France between the second and third semesters.)*
>
> *It is now well known that Prince Friedrich Wilhelm took lively part in university life and thereby developed his ingenious, beautiful affability, and that he entered the military service immediately after his student days, and was then gradually familiarized with the demands of practical civil service, first theoretically and then practically.*

After having obtained the above answers, Darmstadt decided to have Prince Ludwig and Prince Heinrich first gain practical military experience in field service for another year. In the meantime, they had also resolved the second question regarding the choice of university and had decided not for Bonn but for Göttingen. This was done in particular on the advice of Professor Ernst Curtius, the tutor and teacher of Prince Friedrich Wilhelm of Prussia, who had written to his friend *Hofrat* Theodor Becker in Darmstadt the following letter, which is rather interesting:

---

wrote the following remembrance after her stay at Ilinskoe, the country estate of her sister Elisabeth and her husband Sergei, in 1890: '*As Serge knew that Papa and I were interested in archaeological research, he arranged for the opening of three "Kourgan" (funeral mounds) on the Nikolsky property. Pot sherds, bronze bracelets, and armlets, as well as plated necklaces and horse-trappings were found. (...) Papa had been a member of the Hessian Archaeological Society for years and under the guidance of a very able member of it, Mr Kofler, had been present at many excavations to which he used to take us also.*' (Victoria Marchioness of Milford Haven, *Recollections*, 132 of the PDF file)

Dear friend!

You have requested my advice concerning the choice of university for the princes entrusted to your education. I gladly tell you all I can about it; however, it can neither be much, nor important, or decisive, since the personalities in question must be taken into account and that must be the decisive factor.

The first thought falls on Bonn. It is a first-class university, rich in important teachers; as a foundation of recent date, it is less rigid in its traditions than other universities; learning and life permeate each other more easily, if only because of the lively international traffic sailing up and down the Rhine. Moreover, the city's location favours a more rural way of life; on the whole, good manners have kept the rule in Bonn, and the gathering of young people from the north and the south gives one the opportunity to see the various tribes and regions of the German land represented in the core of their youths, here more than elsewhere.

These and other advantages of the Rhine University have led a considerable number of German princely sons to Bonn, especially in recent years. Perhaps this is precisely the main concern that parents of princes might have with regard to Bonn. For it is inevitable that the princes who are present in Bonn at the same time form a kind of circle for themselves; many different claims and suppositions arise from this, which an individual cannot completely evade. Admittedly, these conditions change from one half year to the next, but the most obvious danger in Bonn is that the benefits which a young prince may derive from university life be diminished for him by a circle of peers claiming him for themselves, thereby hindering him from associating with people of his own choosing.

When I mention Göttingen as an institution to consider apart from Bonn, the university of today's princes, I do so first of all based on the experience that Göttingen has recently been rather rejuvenated and refreshed and that there is not much left of the old pedantry. But especially because of the circumstance that Professor Hansen, a man of rare efficiency, is available for Political Economy, as soon as this is to come to the fore. I do not think there is a second man who can introduce a young man in such a practical way to all matters of political economy and national economy as Hansen, whose fresh personality and direct teaching make a great impression; with his rich experience, he is able to impart a great deal of most important knowledge which cannot be found in any textbook.

Apart from Hansen, Waitz seems to me very well suited as a history teacher to introduce the young princes to the deeper understanding of the history of our countries and law.

The consideration of these two men seems to me to carry much weight in favour of Göttingen, although I must confess that Göttingen is far less known to me than Bonn as far as the local life and the dominant tone are concerned.

In Bonn, Professor Perthes in particular is a man who, in my experience, has a rare gift to introduce young princes, who according to the nature of their circumstances usually do not go through a complete faculty study, to the knowledge of constitutional law, and especially to the history of recent German constitutional law in a concise and practical manner. He would have to be given special consideration if the decision is made in favour of Bonn. In addition, Walter is highly recommended for an introduction to Roman law studies.

If there are still questions with regard to which I could give information, I am entirely at your service, if you would like my advice.

I am closing this letter today ... and remain with best regards

Yours faithfully
Ernst Curtius.
Berlin, 6 July 1855

Studies at the Universities of Göttingen and Giessen (1856–1857)

The advice of the experienced historian and archaeologist Ernst Curtius, who had accompanied Prince Friedrich Wilhelm to the university in Bonn in 1849, was gratefully received and gladly followed in Darmstadt. Prince Ludwig of Hesse and his brother Heinrich moved to Göttingen[25] in Easter 1856 to attend the university for a year. They attended Hansen's lectures on political economy and national economy and Professor Waitz's lectures on history. This famous co-worker and later director of the national work *Monumenta Germaniae Historica* had come to Göttingen in 1849 and gathered a very large circle of students there through his lectures, which distinguished themselves by their astute research and excellent form. The two princes regularly attended all the lectures under the guidance of their governor, worked up their notes at home, and enjoyed a happy time as students in informal intercourse with selected fellow students.

They remained in regular contact and frequently corresponded with their relatives in their homeland, Hesse, of which the following reproduction of a letter from their father, Prince Carl of Hesse, is the best proof:

Darmstadt, July 5, 1856
Dear Mr von Grolman!
Many thanks for your letter, which I received on the 21st of the previous month and gave me nothing but joy, like all the news from Göttingen up to now, thank God. It would be very kind of you to purchase the items mentioned as gifts for Heinrich's name day for the 12th; we will send an album, knives, gloves, as well as the two beautiful repeater watches that have arrived from Geneva. Ludwig will be happy to wear the one intended for him in advance and to be given it afterwards as a gift

---

[25] At the time, the city of Göttingen was part of the Kingdom of Hanover.

on the 25th of the next month (Ludwigstag), when the additions to his copperware will await him. Up to now, the Grand Duke has not yet spoken to us about gifts; if he will still do so, we will suggest to him the cigar objects; I am very pleased that the sons still smoke prudently, as it will only benefit their lungs.

Their daily schedule shows a good use of time; we note with pleasure a youthful satisfaction in the children's letters. It is a good thing that they work diligently, and I hope that good results will follow, and that their oral expression of thoughts will gradually improve; this gift is not a strong point of the family, but it can be learned to some extent. The letters are often quite pretty; sometimes one can see that they are written in a hurried manner. Ludwig reports very conscientiously and punctually everything he has experienced, whereas Heinrich seems to have ease in writing and often expresses himself with a certain verve. We will sometimes make our remarks. By the way, it is a great joy for us that our beloved children write so often. It would be nice if the lovely Musica could once again be welcomed and loved by the sons. Heinrich's small landscapes, which he sent us, testify that he has not let his pretty talent slumber completely.

Please give my warmest greetings to the dear sons. I will soon thank Ludwig for his last letter. I will close quickly ... I gratefully remain

        Yours sincerely,
        Carl, Prince of Hesse

The reader may gather from these lines that both princes continued to practice the fine arts during their time at the university. Both Prince Ludwig and Prince Heinrich loved music, both played the piano and had a great understanding of art. In addition, Prince Heinrich was particularly good at drawing. In subsequent years, both rarely practiced music, but they remained interested in classical German music.[26]

---

[26] Ernst Ludwig, Grand Duke Ludwig IV's son, later stated that his father loved the theatre very much and went almost every day. His children accompanied

In the meantime, it had become increasingly probable that Prince Ludwig might one day be called to occupy the Hessian throne: the grand-ducal couple, who had been married for over two decades, had remained childless, and Prince Carl of Hesse, who often suffered from headaches so severe that he could barely think, had already declared that he did not wish to succeed his brother on the throne. In view of the knowledge that a future sovereign would be required to have, it was now believed necessary to extend both the intellectual development of Prince Ludwig and his representative duties as a prince.

In the summer of 1856, as a result of such or similar considerations, Grand Duke Ludwig III commissioned Prince Ludwig of Hesse to represent him at the imperial coronation of Czar Alexander II in Moscow in a similar manner as Prince Friedrich Wilhelm of Prussia had to do for King Friedrich Wilhelm IV.[27] His companions on this first diplomatic journey were Major General and Brigade Commander Baron von Rabenau and his son,[28] a lieutenant in the Guard Chevau-léger Regiment at the time as well as a peer and playmate of the prince. On this occasion, Emperor Alexander II honoured the prince by appointing him colonel-in-chief of the 6th Russian Hussar Regiment 'Kliastitsy'[29] on the eve of Prince Ludwig's nineteenth birthday (that is, on 11 September 1856).[30] The prince returned to

---

him often. His father loved music and frequently attended concerts and operas, but was not musically trained at all. His favourite opera was *'Fidelio'*. (Ernst Ludwig Grossherzog von Hessen und bei Rhein, *Erinnertes*, 125 and 49.)

[27] The coronation took place on 7 September 1856. The Czar's predecessor, Nicholas I, had died of pneumonia on 2 March 1855.

[28] Friedrich Baron von Nordeck zur Rabenau (1793–1863), Major General and Commander of the First Infantry Brigade. The son referred to by Zernin was presumably Ferdinand Karl Baron von Nordeck zur Rabenau (1837–1892).

[29] [Note by G. Zernin:] In 1898, after the conversion of almost all Russian cavalry regiments into dragoon regiments, this regiment was called '18th Dragoon Regiment'.

[30] Cf. Vladislav Pavlovitch Tsekhanovetskiy. *Istoriya 18 Dragunskogo*

his home country with more mature views and a wider perspective.

In the spring of 1857, after their one-year stay in Göttingen, both princes enrolled at the State University of Giessen to attend various lectures during the summer semester. Just as in Göttingen, they primarily attended lectures on constitutional law and history, which were supplemented with other academic lectures on subjects in which they were particularly interested. They left Giessen before the beginning of the summer holidays and returned to Darmstadt, where they were promoted to captains on Ludwigstag – 25 August 1857.

Once again, the princes entered military service. They were each assigned a company in the 1st Grand-ducal Hessian (Lifeguards) Regiment and undertook front service like any other captain and company commander. Both of them were eager to meet all the demands made on them – and these were not small in number and importance – and to satisfy the demands of their superiors; they also maintained loyal comradeship with their comrades in arms and acquired numerous supporters and even trusted friends in their ranks. They shared the joys and sorrows of the exercises with their men and were rather affable in their dealings with them.

Klyastitskogo ego korolevskogo vysotchestva velikogo gertsoga Gessenskogo polka: 1806–1886 (Warsaw: Tipografiya brat'ev Ezhinskikh, 1886), 271. According to Tsekhanovetskiy, the colonel-in-chief of this regiment was 'Prince Ludwig of Hesse' from 30 August 1856 until his death; this Julian calendar date corresponds with the Gregorian calendar date of 11 September 1856. Prince Ludwig was succeeded by his son, Grand Duke Ernst Ludwig of Hesse, who was the colonel-in-chief of this regiment from 1892 until the beginning of World War I.

Entry into the Prussian military service (1859)

At the end of the fifties and the beginning of the sixties [of the nineteenth century], the Grand-ducal Court of Darmstadt, as well as the Hessian government circles, had a marked preference for Austrian politics and the Austrian imperial army under the glorious black-and-yellow banner. Therefore, it often happened that sons of good Hessian families sought and easily found their way into the Austrian army. Grand Duke Ludwig III probably also wished to see his nephews, Princes Ludwig and Heinrich, to continue their military training in the Austrian army, in which his own brother, Prince Alexander of Hesse,[31] had reached the rank of major general and brigade commander at that time. On the other hand, Princess Carl of Hessen, the mother of the princes had always wished that her two sons would undergo the tried and tested Prussian military school, from which her own father, Prince Wilhelm of Prussia, had come. She found substantial support for her view in her consultations with Prussia's former envoy to the Federal Convention of the German Confederation in Frankfurt am Main – Otto von Bismarck-Schönhausen.[32] The details of these processes have not yet become generally known, but they appear rather important to us and we go into them a little more closely here.

---

[31] In 1851, Prince Alexander of Hesse (1823–1888) had married Countess Julia Hauke (1825–1895). She was granted the title Countess of Battenberg in 1851 and Princess of Battenberg in 1858. Thus, Prince Alexander of Hesse became the founding father of the Battenberg/Mountbatten family. Their son Prince Alexander of Battenberg (1857–1893) became the tsar of Bulgaria. Their son Prince Ludwig of Battenberg (1854–1921) married Princess Victoria (1863–1950), the oldest daughter of Prince Ludwig of Hesse and by Rhine and Princess Alice of the United Kingdom.

[32] Otto von Bismarck-Schönhausen (1815–1898), the subsequent chancellor of the German Empire.

First, we find in Volume 15 of the publications of the Royal Prussian State Archives arranged and supported by the Royal Archive Administration – which deals with Prussia in the Federal Convention in 1851–1859[33] – documents of the Royal Prussian Legation to the Federal Convention, edited by Dr Ritter von Poschinger. In particular, page 466 of Part 3 provides the following *Immediat* message regarding the entry of two grand-ducal Hessian princes in the Prussian army on 30 December 1858:

On the occasion of the festivities in Darmstadt[34], I (Herr von Bismarck) have received Princess Carl of Hesse in a special audience, during which she discussed with me the immediate future of her sons, Prince Ludwig and Prince Heinrich. Her Royal Highness treated the departure of both princes to Potsdam for their entry into the 1st Foot Guard Regiment as a foregone conclusion, although this intention remained partially unknown and partially questioned in the official circles of Darmstadt. The Grand Duke had initially objected to the plan, stating that it was out of line with his general policy. His Royal Highness attached the highest importance to the relations with Prussia, but could 'not offend Austria'; therefore at least one of the two princes should go into imperial (Austrian) service. Her Royal Highness Princess Carl then urgently asked not to separate the two young gentlemen and expressed concern about the influence that Austrian garrison life in small, frequently changing provincial towns must have on the princes when they devote themselves to the military profession with the seriousness that is desired. Her Royal Highness's objection to the proposal of Prince Alexander[35] to take one of his nephews into his Italian garrison was that the views which the princes would gain there, from the point of view of

---

[33] *Publicationen aus den Königlich Preußischen Staatsarchiven, veranlaßt und unterstützt durch die Königliche Archivverwaltung. Vol. 15, Preußen im Bundestag 1851–59.*

[34] [Note by G. Zernin:] Grand Duke Ludwig III of Hesse and Grand Duchess Mathilde celebrated their silver wedding anniversary on 26 December 1858.

[35] [Note by G. Zernin:] Prince Alexander of Hesse stood as an Austrian brigade commander in Milan at that time.

the Austrian military, did not constitute an appropriate training that would prepare them for the profession of a German prince, whereas they would get to know and study conditions more similar to those at home in Prussia; moreover, she also considered it important to attach importance to the protection, supervision, and goodwill that the princes would certainly enjoy in the vicinity of the Prussian Court. She also stated that she knew no officer corps in the whole world in the company of which she would see her sons with more peace of mind than that of our Guards in general, but especially of the regiment in Potsdam. Her maternal concern and eloquence seem to have won a decisive victory over the political views; at least, Her Royal Highness told me that the Grand Duke, when he was in Vienna, prepared the [Austrian] Emperor for the entry of both gentlemen into the Prussian army, but would have promised that Prince Wilhelm – the youngest nephew of His Royal Highness – would enter into the Austrian service in the future. Ultimately, the determining factor for His Royal Highness was consideration for the wishes of both parents of the princes, but only after Her Royal Highness the Grand Duchess had overcome her dislike of the plan. The plan would already have been brought to its actual fulfilment, if the change of cabinet which we had made did not give the Austrian influences at the court an excuse to delay, by claiming that they first had to wait and see how Prussia's policy towards the rest of Germany would develop. Meanwhile, as I have said, the Princess spoke of the entry of the princes into the 1st Guard Regiment as of a fact to which only the approval of the Prince Regent[36] *was to be requested and would be sought without delay.*

This *Immediat* report is, as we have seen, dated 30 December 1858. Grand Duke Ludwig III sent the following handwritten letter to His Royal Highness the Prince Regent of Prussia on 16 January 1859:

---

[36] Prince Wilhelm of Prussia (1799–1888) was Prince Regent of the Kingdom of Prussia from 7 October 1858, representing his brother King Friedrich Wilhelm IV of Prussia, who was ill. He succeeded his brother as King Wilhelm I of Prussia after the death of King Friedrich Wilhelm IV on 2 January 1861.

You have already been informed through Elisabeth[37] that it will be a great pleasure to me to see my two nephews, Ludwig and Heinrich, enter the excellent Prussian army. As I hear now that you want to admit these two good young people, who already have had a good military education, I hurry to thank you for this new proof of your friendship and love for me and my House from the bottom of my heart.

General Schäffer,[38] whom you know very well, will bring you these lines; he knows the Prussian army and our circumstances, as well as my nephews, very well and I ask you to allow him to present to you my wishes in this regard personally and to trust him as he deserves.

You have certainly been convinced, my dear Wilhelm, that I have taken the most heartfelt sympathy in all that has so grievously affected you and your family through the severe illness of the dear and beloved king. I know your faithful fraternal heart and wish nothing more than to hear only good about you and your health through Schäffer.

I ask you to recommend me warmly and with affection to your dearly esteemed wife, and to keep your ever so friendly attitude towards me always unchanged.

Your faithful cousin and friend, Ludwig[39]

Two answers to this handwritten letter promptly arrived from Berlin – one official answer and one personal in the form of a handwritten letter, the former dated 22 January 1859 and the latter dated 25 January 1859. They were worded in the following manner:

---

[37] [Note by G. Zernin:] Princess Carl of Hesse.
[38] [Note by G. Zernin:] General of the Infantry Baron von Schäffer-Bernstein, Grand-ducal Hessian Minister of War.
[39] [Note by G. Zernin:] The following words were written by the orderly Grand Duke Ludwig III on the large blue envelope to this letter, which is kept in the Darmstadt Court and State Archives: *Letter to the Prince Regent of Prussia about the entry of my nephews Ludwig and Heinrich into the Prussian army. Expedited 16.1.59.*

I.

To the Grand Duke of Hesse and by Rhine, Royal Highness.

Most Serene Sovereign, dear cousin and brother!

In your kind letter dated the 16th of this month that was presented to me by the General Adjutant General of the Infantry and Minister of War, Baron von Schäffer-Bernstein, Your Royal Highness has expressed the wish that I allow the entry of Your Royal Highness's nephews, Grand-ducal Highnesses Prince Ludwig and Prince Heinrich of Hesse and by Rhine, into the Prussian military service. I am particularly pleased to see that Your Royal Highness, as well as the Most Serene Parents of the two princes, have decided to present the latter to the Prussian army for military service for their further education. It is with the utmost obligingness that I hereby fulfil the wish of Your Royal Highness by appointing the two grand-ducal princes as captains à la suite of the 1st Foot Guard Regiment, in which His Majesty the King, as well as my brothers and I also began our military careers, and I have given further orders accordingly.

On this occasion, Your Royal Highness, please receive the assurance of the true respect and friendship with which I remain,

Your Royal Highness's friendly cousin and brother
Wilhelm, Prince Regent of Prussia.
Berlin, 22 January 1859

II.

Berlin, 25 January 1859

With great joy I have inferred from your private and official letters the realization of the wishes that Elisabeth had already expressed to me. I can only repeat that it is our greatest pleasure to see your two nephews enter into our army and that it will be my conscientious duty to train them, according to your wish, to become efficient soldiers without harming their other qualities.

General of the Infantry von Schäffer, whom I greatly enjoyed seeing *here on such a pleasing occasion, will have told you that both princes are to be sent to the Fusilier Battalion 1st Guard Regiment, the commander of which will be their special mentor, while the company chiefs will, of course, have to take on the special training. Since your nephews are captains, they cannot be deployed in one and the same company, because otherwise they would not be properly occupied. It is true that Major von Kessel[40] has been Commander of the Fusilier Battalion for a very short time, but he has received many flattering remarks and we believe he is one of our most distinguished young staff officers.*

So nothing stands in the way of the arrival of your nephews anymore. Laying me at the feet of the Grand Duchess and thanking you warmly for your dear sympathy for my difficult office,

Your faithful cousin Wilhelm.

My wife extends her warmest regards to you.

The letter is reproduced verbatim here and is evidently written out of Prince Regent Wilhelm's heart's desire and entirely by himself.

* * *

All the difficulties had now been eliminated, and all preparations had been made so that the princes, who had already been appointed as captains à la suite of the 1st Foot Guard Regiment by supreme cabinet order of 22 January 1859, could move to Potsdam. It is well known that the Potsdam Guard Parade had already distinguished itself before the Seven Years' War[41] by its unyieldingness in the service and has preserved its honourable traditions up to the present day. Added to this was Major von

---

[40] [Note by G. Zernin:] He died later as general of the infantry. He was also the father of the current major general and commander of the 1st Guard Infantry Brigade.

[41] The Seven Years' War was fought in Europe, North-America, Africa, and Asia from 1756 to 1763.

Kessel's strict sense of duty, which compelled the two Hessian princes to make every effort to live up to the expectations placed on them. A new drill book had to be learned; an unfamiliar service regulation had to be precisely practiced; teams of a different kind of people with unfamiliar expressions, different manners and customs had to be led, guided, and trained. In brief, all kinds of difficulties had to be overcome.

The princes succeeded in doing so, not all at once, but gradually. A very detailed report written by the Grand-ducal Hessian envoy to the court of Berlin, Count von Görtz,[42] dated 24 February 1860, to his native government on the basis of communications from the Colonel and then Chief of the General Staff of the Guards Corps, Baron von Berg, mentioned the following particularly significant points:

The princes are generally respected and popular for their exemplary morality and benevolent and undemanding behaviour. Their eagerness to train themselves in the military and to fulfil their official duties is impeccable, and they stand out favourably from many other young gentlemen of their rank. Until now, their independent achievements that were most appreciated were those in the context of the special assignments that were given to them during last year's manoeuvres; they were more satisfied with their performances on these occasions than with their leadership of companies, which was assigned to them by way of trial for a period of about fourteen days; the independent constant care for detail and the independent attitude towards non-commissioned officers with service experience left much to be desired here. ...

Incidentally, both princes do not yet consider themselves capable of taking on the independent leadership of companies at the moment. ...

The princes live very economically and sparingly; it made therefore a particularly favourable impression when they gave each of their companies a gift of 50 thalers at Christmas. ...

---

[42] Carl, Count von Schlitz genannt von Görtz (1822–1885).

Engagement (1860) and marriage (1862)

After both Prince Ludwig and his brother Prince Heinrich had attained a certain confidence in their life in the Prussian army and had also become familiar with the court in Berlin, where they were always regarded as welcome guests, they decided to undertake further journeys in order to become personally acquainted with other European courts. In the summer of 1860, the brothers simultaneously took leave to go to England together and introduce themselves to the Royal Family in Windsor. Both princes enjoyed a rather courteous welcome there and liked their new surroundings very much. The 17-year-old Princess Alice of the United Kingdom immediately made a deep impression on Prince Ludwig, while the Queen's daughter was quite taken with the fresh, masculine, and natural character of the then heir to the Hessian throne. The parents of both young people met in Mainz a few weeks later, whereupon Prince Ludwig hurried to Windsor for the second time. As *'the Queen and the Prince … saw in the young Prince the qualities which satisfied them that they might entrust their daughter to his care without misgiving'*,[43] as the author Sir Theodore Martin reported in *The Life of the Prince Consort*, a mutual agreement was made which was soon followed by an official engagement on 30 November 1860.

Queen Victoria personally wrote the following interesting account of how the engagement came about in her journal:

'After dinner, while talking to the gentlemen, I perceived Alice and Louis talking before the fireplace more earnestly than usual, and, when I passed to go to the other room, both came up to me, and Alice in much agitation said that he had proposed to her, and he begged for my blessing. I could only squeeze his hand, and say "Certainly," and that we would see him in our room later. Got through the evening, working as well as

---

[43] Theodore Martin, *The Life of His Royal Highness The Prince Consort*, Vol. V (New York: Appleton & Co., 1880), 211.

we could. Alice came to our room, … agitated but quiet. … Albert sent for Louis to his room – went first to him, and then called Alice and me in. … Louis has a warm, noble heart. We embraced our dear Alice and praised her much to him. He pressed and kissed my hand, and I embraced him. After talking a little we parted; a most touching, and to me most sacred moment.'[44]

A joyful and happy time followed for the young bridal couple. In particular, the Queen's stay with her family and Prince Ludwig at Balmoral in September 1861 was a source of pure enjoyment for all participants. They roamed the splendid area of the Scottish Highlands in all directions and combined their explorations with successful hunting expeditions. Thus the Royal Family and their dear guest often undertook long excursions – for example to Invermark and Fettercairn, to Loch Avon, Glen Fishie, Dalwhinnie and Blair Athole, and finally to the top of Cairn Turc and Cairn Glaishie, in the course of which the great scenic beauties of the incomparable area were enjoyed in quite a leisurely manner.[45] Queen Victoria wrote about one of these trips to Blair Athole in her journal:

'This was the pleasantest and most enjoyable expedition I ever made; and the recollection of it will always be most agreeable to me, and increase my wish to make more! Was so glad dear Louis (who is a charming companion) was with us. Have enjoyed nothing as much, or indeed felt so much cheered by anything, since my great sorrow.[46] *Did not feel tired.'*[47]

---

[44] [Note by G. Zernin:] Theodore Martin, *The Life of His Royal Highness The Prince Consort*, Vol. V (New York: D. Appleton & Co., 1880), 212.

[45] Victoria Queen of the United Kingdom and Arthur Helps, *Leaves from the Journal of Our Life in the Highlands: From 1848 to 1861; Earlier Visits to Scotland, and Tours in England and Ireland and Yachting Excursions* (London: Smith, Elder, 1868), 214, 221, 222, 238, 239.

[46] The Queen's mother, the Duchess of Kent, died on 16 March 1861.

[47] [Note by G. Zernin:] Victoria Queen of the United Kingdom and Arthur Helps, *Leaves from the Journal of Our Life in the Highlands*, 236.

In the meantime, Prince Ludwig, like his brother Heinrich, continued his education at the military academy in Potsdam diligently. They attended the large-scale exercises of the Guards Corps in the summer of 1860 and the summer of 1861, and the Prince Regent, or King Wilhelm I, was very pleased with their achievements. The promotion of both of them to the rank of major, which took place on the day of the coronation of King Wilhelm I in Königsberg on 18 October 1861, must be regarded as an obvious proof of this; Prince Ludwig had only just turned 24 years of age. After he had participated in the inspections of the Guards Corps near Potsdam and Berlin in the spring of 1862, he was allowed to consider his training in the Prussian military service as complete and returned to his home country, Hesse.

The marriage of Prince Ludwig to the second daughter of the English Queen had been planned for the year 1861, but had to be postponed three times because of three deaths: first the death of the abovementioned Duchess of Kent, then the death of Prince Albert on 14 December 1861, followed by the death of Grand Duchess Mathilde of Hesse in Darmstadt on 25 May 1862. In view of these events, it was decided to dispense with the usual grand festivities – such as those which usually take place when a daughter of the English Queen marries – and to celebrate the wedding privately. Thus, on 1 July 1862, the Archbishop of York joined the hands of the two princely children in matrimony at Osborne House on the Isle of Wight, whereupon the newly-wed couple left English soil a few days later to make their festive entry into the Grand-ducal Hessian residence on 12 July 1862. '*As this was entirely a marriage of affection, the happiness of the "young people" was very great.*' These words from the biography of the young wife of the Hessian prince were to prove true from then on.[48]

---

[48] [Note by G. Zernin:] Alice Grand Duchess of Hesse, *Alice*, 25.

Activity in the Hessian military service (1862–1866)

Prince Ludwig of Hesse, who had been promoted by Grand Duke Ludwig III of Hesse to colonel and second colonel-in-chief of the Grand-ducal Hessian Guard Chevau-léger Regiment (today 1st Grand-ducal Hessian Guard Dragoon Regiment No. 23) shortly before his marriage, on 9 June 1862, found much work in his new position. He did not merely want the title of colonel and regimental commander but also wanted to really be one. Not only did he quickly familiarize himself with the professional duties of a cavalry troop commander but he also sought to improve his native military service in all branches of the armed forces wherever and however he could. He resolutely opposed abuses and old impractical traditions, and he was not afraid to fight the views of superiors if he could not approve of them; at one point, he even felt compelled to offer his resignation when one of his well-founded demands appeared to be unable to get through. But Grand Duke Ludwig III had a just mind and complied with the requests that Prince Ludwig had made at that time.

The prince could best recover from all the efforts and troubles of daily service in the quiet rooms of his family home and it was well-deserved praise that his own wife paid him tribute when she wrote the following lines to her mother, Queen Victoria, on 30 June 1863:

'*To-morrow is our dear wedding-day. With what gratitude do I look back to that commencement of such happiness, and such real and true love, which even daily increases in my beloved husband! (...) Oh, dear Mama, if you only knew how excellent he is! I wish I were good like him, for he is free from any selfish, small, or uncharitable feelings. You should see how he is beloved by all his people.*'[49]

---

[49] [Note by G. Zernin:] Alice Grand Duchess of Hesse, *Alice*, 58.

Participation in the Campaign of the Main (1866)

This quiet, friendly life was suddenly interrupted in the spring of 1866.[50] War broke out between Prussia on the one hand and Austria and its southern German allies on the other. Hesse sided with the latter. Prince Ludwig, who had already been promoted to major general on 3 September 1865, was now in command of the Grand-ducal Hessian Cavalry Brigade and took to the field at the head of the two Hessian cavalry regiments. It was with a heavy heart that he bid farewell to his wife and children and went to war.[51] The first and bloodiest battle fought by the Hessians in this campaign was the one at Frohnhofen-Laufach[52] on 13 July. The village of Frohnhofen was occupied by Prussian troops of the

---

[50] Shortly after the end of the Prusso-Danish War on 30 October 1864, a dispute arose between the Kingdom of Prussia and the Austrian Empire over the joint administration of Schleswig-Holstein, which they had seized from Denmark. The conflict escalated into the Austrian-Prussian War in June 1866. The then reigning Grand Duke of Hesse and by Rhine, Ludwig III, sided with Austria as did the Grand Duchy of Baden and the kingdoms of Bavaria, Württemberg, and Saxony. Prussia was the winner of this war. The first truce between Prussia and Austria was reached on 22 July, followed by the Armistice of Nikolsburg on 26 July, and the Peace Treaty of Prague on 23 August of 1866. The allies of Austria also reached armistices with Prussia. The armistice between the Grand Duchy of Hesse and by Rhine and Prussia on 1 August 1866 resulted in a peace treaty on 3 September 1866. Under the peace treaty between Prussia and Austria, the German Confederation was dissolved and Prussia held the dutchies of Schleswig and Holstein, the Electorate of Hesse (or Hesse-Kassel), the Free City of Frankfurt, and more. Under the peace treaty between Prussia and the Grand Duchy of Hesse and by Rhine, Hesse had to pay reparations to Prussia and was forced to cede both the former landgraviate of Hesse-Homburg and the Hessian Hinterland to Prussia.

[51] Prince Ludwig's wife wrote about her concerns for her husband and her worries about the war in general in her letters to her mother, Queen Victoria. See Alice Grand Duchess of Hesse, *Alice*, 138–159.

[52] Frohnhofen is a small village to the west of Laufach in the district of Aschaffenburg (Bavaria).

Brigade of von Wrangel[53] and was to be taken by the Hessians in the late afternoon. With drums beating, first the 1st Hessian Infantry (Life Guard) Regiment, supported by a battery, then the 3rd, and finally also the 4th Infantry Regiment proceeded with determination against the village; the troops took its fence by themselves in the first attack, but could not hold their own against the continuous rapid fire from the needle rifles. Robbed of most of their officers, the companies that had been shot down finally had to retreat; they withdrew in good order to Aschaffenburg. The troops and, with them, Prince Ludwig of Hesse were also involved in the Battles of Aschaffenburg and Gerchsheim[54], but here too they could not carry off the palm of victory. However, the gallant prince did succeed in setting a shining example of personal courage in the two battles on 14 and 25 July as well as in demonstrating an adequate understanding of the orders required at critical moments. Having been promoted to lieutenant general and commander of the Grand-ducal Hessian Division on 13 August 1866, the prince returned home in September.[55]

---

[53] Karl von Wrangel (1812–1899), a Prussian General of the Infantry.

[54] Gerchsheim is a village in the northeast of the Grand Duchy of Baden. The Battle of Aschaffenburg took place on 14 July 1866, the Battle of Gerchsheim on 25 July 1866.

[55] [Note by G. Zernin:] More about the participation of Prince Ludwig of Hesse in the Campaign of the Main can be found in the following two works:

1) *Der Antheil der Großherzoglich Hessischen Armee-Division am Kriege 1866* by von Zimmermann, lieutenant colonel in the Great General Staff (*Kriegsgeschichtliche Einzelschriften, herausgegeben vom großen Generalstabe, Abtheilung für Kriegsgeschichte*, Heft 22 and Heft 23). *Mit einer Uebersichtskarte, 4 Pläne und 4 Skizze.* Berlin: E. S. Mittler & Sohn, 1897. This work of military history was commissioned by His Royal Highness, the now ruling Grand Duke Ernst Ludwig of Hesse and by Rhine.

2) *Die Operationen des VIII. deutschen Bundes-Corps im Feldzuge des Jahres 1866. Nach authentischen Quellen dargestellt* by von Baur, lieutenant general in the army of the Kingdom of Württemberg. *Mit 10 Beilagen.* Darmstadt and Leipzig: Eduard Zernin, 1868.

The entire division now looked with full confidence to its new leader; they had fought in the preceding campaign unsuccessfully, but with well-known Old Hessian bravery, and they hoped to be able to fight with more luck under the command of their young princely commander, who had just proved himself in such an excellent manner, in a new war, which was already foreseen at that time.[56]

On 7 May 1867, Hesse concluded its first military convention with Prussia. Under this convention, Prince Ludwig was confirmed as commander of the Grand-ducal Hessian (25th) Division on 1 October 1867. With the help of capable domestic and foreign forces – among the latter, Major General von Wittich, who was sent from Prussia to Darmstadt, must be mentioned in particular – he was now most eager to perfect the military training of the troops under his command and to make them fully ready for a new campaign. The extent to which he succeeded in accomplishing this task was clearly revealed in the period that followed.

---

[56] After the war of 1866, a new confederation under the leadership of the Kingdom of Prussia came into existence: the North German Confederation. The federal constitution was adopted on 1 July 1867. Of the Grand Duchy of Hesse and by Rhine only the province of Upper Hesse joined this new confederation. The Kingdoms of Bavaria and Württemberg and the Grand Duchy of Baden remained outside of this new confederation for the time being.

By 1870, the French Empire feared that Prussia and the North German Confederation would become too powerful and a threat to France. Emperor Napoleon III of the French was also confronted with demands for democratic reforms and believed that a war with Prussia and potential territorial gains could help secure support for the Bonaparte dynasty in his country. Simultaneously, Otto von Bismarck, the Federal Chancellor of the North German Confederation, felt that a war between Prussia and France was necessary to persuade the southern German states to side with Prussia and join the North German Confederation.

Participation in the Franco-German War (1870–1871)

In the hot summer of 1870, the Franco-German war broke out.[57] King Wilhelm ordered the mobilisation of the entire German army on 16 July, and the troops of the 25th Division set off on their march across the Rhine and through the Palatinate to France on 25 July. Prince Ludwig of Hesse stood at the head of this division, similar to how his illustrious ancestor Prince Emil of Hesse had led the Hessian troops against the arch-enemy in 1814 and 1815. Prince Ludwig had silently vowed to fight bravely for the welfare of his fatherland and the honour of Hesse – the gallant leader kept this promise.

He parted from his family with a heavy heart. His wife wrote the following about their farewell on 26 July:

'I parted with dear Louis late in the evening [of 25 July], on the high road outside the village in which he was quartered for the night

---

[57] When Spain offered the vacant Spanish throne to Prince Leopold of Hohenzollern-Sigmaringen in February 1870, France protested against this association between the House of Hohenzollern and Spain. Although Prince Leopold declined the offer, France demanded a guarantee from King Wilhelm I of Prussia that the House of Hohenzollern would not aspire to this position in the future either. This demand was presented to the king by the French ambassador to Prussia during an informal meeting in the town of Bad Ems in Hesse-Nassau on 13 July 1870. The king politely refused to provide such a guarantee and had a dispatch regarding this meeting sent to Federal Chancellor Otto von Bismarck. Bismarck cunningly made the contents of the dispatch public in a press release, laying out the matter in clear terms, but he phrased it in an undiplomatic manner, which made the Germans believe that the French ambassador had insulted their king and made the French believe that their ambassador had been insulted. Emotions ran so high that France declared war on Germany on 19 July 1870. This time, the Kingdoms of Bavaria and Württemberg and the Grand Duchies of Hesse and by Rhine and Baden, which had remained outside of the North German Confederation, sided with Prussia and eventually joined the Confederation in November 1870. After the accession of these four southern German states, the Confederation was renamed the German Empire on 10 December 1870.

[Gernsheim, Hesse], *and we looked back until nothing more was to be seen of each other. May the Almighty watch over his precious life, and bring him safe back again: all the pain and anxiety are forgotten and willingly borne if he is only left to me and to his children!'*[58]

The Almighty fulfilled the high-born lady's wish and graciously protected the life and health of Prince Ludwig; however, he had to face grave dangers during the long war. The following are the individual days of battle and times when bullets rained upon the prince at the head of his brave troops:
- Battle of Vionville-Mars-la-Tour on 16 August 1870
- Battle of Gravelotte-St. Privat on 18 August 1870
- Encirclement of Metz from 19 August to 27 October 1870
- Battle of Noisseville on 31 August and 1 September 1870
- Battle of Orléans on 3 and 4 December 1870
- Battle of Beaugency-Cravant, especially at Les Trois Cheminées[59] on 8 December 1870
- Battle of Montlivault and Chambord on 9 December 1870
- Battle of Vienne[60] on 10 December 1870

In particular, the Hessian division's days of glory in this war were 18 August 1870 near Metz and 9 December 1870, the latter because of the seizure of Chambord Castle. In the former battle, no less than 86 officers, 137 non-commissioned officers, and 1,446 men died or were wounded on the Hessian side. On the day of the Battle of Chambord, only a very small portion of the troops – exactly 54 men of the 4th Infantry Regiment under Captain Kattrein – took the castle by storm, wherein 250 Frenchmen and

---

[58] [Note by G. Zernin:] Alice Grand Duchess of Hesse, *Alice*, 251.
[59] Les Trois Cheminées ('The Three Chimneys') presumably refers to a hamlet a few kilometres southeast of Beaugency in the commune of Lailly-en-Val in the Loiret department. Lailly-en-Val was badly damaged by Prussian troops in 1870. A central building in this hamlet, at the junction of the Rue du Val and the main Route de Blois, has three chimneys.
[60] This refers to Blois-Vienne, the south-eastern part of Blois on the left bank of the River Loire.

5 guns were captured, so that this troop, with just pride, was allowed to write the following words in the dome of the castle: *'Ce château défendu par 3300 Français, fût pris par 54 soldats hessois, qui emmenaient 5 pièces de canon et 250 prisonniers.'* With good reason, the meeting of Prince Ludwig of Hesse with King Wilhelm I of Prussia on the evening of the day of the battle on 18 August and the storming of Chambord Castle by Captain Kattrein and his 54 soldiers were selected as the subjects of the two reliefs on the state war memorial inaugurated in Darmstadt on 18 August 1879.[61]

---

[61] [Note by G. Zernin:] There are numerous proofs of the fearlessness and disregard for death of Prince Ludwig of Hesse under the enemy's fire, of which only a few can be mentioned here – for example, the following eyewitness account:

On 18 August 1870, during the march of the regiments into the line of battle, His Royal Highness the Grand Duke, at that time Commander of the 25th Division, came with his staff in front of the 1st Rifle Battalion in order to indicate its position in the battle line. During this short period of time, the battalion commander, Major Lautenberger – who was behind the battalion – was killed by shrapnel, as were some of the riflemen of the battalion. His Royal Highness the Grand Duke immediately gave orders to follow him with the words: 'Battalion, follow me!' Then, the battalion followed His Royal Highness the Grand Duke in a rapid march to a forest aisle, where he remained, and directed the battalion into it. When there was a stagnation at the entrance of the aisle, His Royal Highness the Grand Duke shouted 'Forward, onward!' with a cheering voice into the column and gave orders with the following words: 'Sergeants, stay and drive all into it!'

On 10 December 1870, during the battle at Vienne, a suburb of Blois, His Royal Highness the Grand Duke dismounted from his horse and stood beside a gun advanced on the embankment [of the River Loire] *to watch its fire effect. As shots were still coming from Blois, despite the white flag being held up there, His Royal Highness said to the battery boss standing next to him: 'Let's aim for the church tower, if those over there do not want to stop shooting!' After a few shots in this direction, the fire stopped. During this time, His Royal Highness the Grand Duke stood in a completely uncovered position, while everyone else sought cover.*

Even in the Battle of Montlivault, Prince Ludwig of Hesse preserved the greatest determination and cool-headedness even in the most dangerous moments. An eyewitness reports about this in the following manner:

Prince Ludwig personally remained in the foremost battle line and distributed

The details of this great war and the achievements of the Hessian troops during the war are described in detail in the well-known work which was written by two fellow combatants in the campaign and published in print by order of Prince and subsequently Grand Duke Ludwig IV of Hesse.[62]

---

the infantrymen on the walls and houses. Prince Wilhelm also found an opportunity to successfully assist his brother in encouraging the troops to persevere at this critical moment.

(H. Scherf and A. Draudt, *Die Theilnahme der Großherzoglich Hessischen (25.) Division an dem Feldzug 1870–71 gegen Frankreich*, Vol. 2, 456.)

Another eyewitness reports the following incident, which we wish to cite as evidence of the genuine comradely behaviour and affable helpfulness of His Grand-ducal Highness:

On the road from Orléans to Blois, which at that time (in December 1870) was very soggy and depleted, I had got stuck in the middle of the road with my somewhat overloaded vehicle and tired, half-starved little horse. After long, futile attempts, I had given up hope of getting further, when, to my horror, I saw marching columns approach from afar on the dead-straight road. I soon noticed a large staff in front. It was early morning. My embarrassment grew by the minute, because after many attempts to free it, the cart stood right across the road and was now blocking it. About fifteen paces in front of the staff, a young general rode alone; I did not know him. I walked up to him and reported my misfortune. 'Where do you want to go?', he asked. 'To Blois,' I answered. And he continued immediately, 'I to Orléans, but you, little gentleman, prevent my whole division from doing that.' The general turned his horse to the column still further back. The staff was grouped at a respectful distance; then, it began to dawn on me. Soon I recognized the Hessian infantry – big, powerful figures. 'Then help free the cart quickly!' The giants immediately grabbed the spokes; I was free in a few seconds, and so was the prince. I wanted to say thank you, but I did not immediately find the right form of address. The prince, who was ahead of me, said: 'I had a greater interest in getting you going again than you had. Now, good journey!' The prince continued his way smiling.

This is what Captain Fritz Hoenig reports in his book *Der Volkskrieg an der Loire im Herbst 1870, 5. Band, die entscheidenden Tage von Orléans im Herbst 1870, 3. Theil, die Auflösung des französischen Heeres vor Orléans (der 3. December 1870) mit 5 Kartenbeilagen* (Berlin: Ernst Siegfried Mittler & Sohn, Königliche Hofbuchhandlung, 1897), 122.

[62] [Note by G. Zernin:] Cf. H. Scherf and A. Draudt, *Die Theilnahme der Großherzoglich Hessischen (25.) Division an dem Feldzuge 1870–71 gegen Frankreich. Auf Allerhöchste Veranlassung Seiner Königlichen Hoheit des*

For his achievements in this war, the prince was awarded the Iron Cross, 2nd class and 1st class, the Hessian and Mecklenburg Military Merit Crosses, the Russian Order of St. George 3rd class, and the High Order Pour le Mérite. On his return to his homeland, he was appointed Chief of the Hessian Infantry Regiment No. 81 in Berlin on 16 June 1871, where he had personally rushed to take part in the triumphal march of the troops into the German capital. On 18 August of the same year, he was appointed Royal Prussian Lieutenant General – the first anniversary of the Battle of Gravelotte-St. Privat. In general, the then Emperor Wilhelm I proved to be extremely kind and benevolent towards the prince, whose military prowess he had come to know and appreciate during the war. Thus, the same Emperor, who had barely just returned from France to Berlin himself, sent him the following telegram on 14 March 1871: *After you have completed the campaign with honour, I grant you a short leave of absence to join your family. Your superiors have been notified. Wilhelm.* Consequently, the prince hurried to Germany to see his family again. He returned to France very soon, only to come back and make his ceremonial entry into Darmstadt at the head of the Grand-ducal Hessian (25th) Division. For this occasion, the entire city was adorned in the most festive manner. The prince was received at a splendid gate of honour in Neckarstrasse and welcomed with a poetic speech. He then expressed his thanks in simple words and led the troops with rich wreaths in a parade march past Grand Duke Ludwig III on Paradeplatz – almost at the same place where the equestrian monument of Grand Duke Ludwig IV currently stands.[63]

Großherzogs Ludwig IV. von Hessen und bei Rhein und auf Grund officieller Acten dargestellt. Mit 16 Skizzen und 12 Karten. Darmstadt, 2 Volumes. 1877/1883.

[63] The Franco-Prussian War ended on 28 January 1871. Prussia and its allies were the victors. The Treaty of Frankfurt was signed on 10 May 1871. France had to cede large parts of Alsace and Lorraine to the German Empire.

Leadership of the Grand-ducal Hessian Division
(1870–1877)

Peace finally reigned again in the country, and Prince Ludwig could finally think about resuming his life as a family man and recovering from the great efforts of the campaign. He visited the seaside resort of Blankenberghe, Belgium, with his wife and children in August and went to England in September to visit Queen Victoria; invigorated, he returned to Darmstadt over the Channel and again took command of the Grand-ducal Hessian Division, the peacetime training of which was rather dear to his heart. After all, it was important to remain on guard against a prostrate but restless and agitated neighbour and to keep the instrument of battle – the army – sharp, so that it was ready for any sudden breach of peace.[64]

The following years brought the prince outer peace, but a lot of inner work. The military convention between Hesse and Prussia that was concluded on 15 June 1871 was enforced and required a rearrangement of the Grand-ducal Hessian (25th) Division. Moreover, Prince Ludwig had the honour of being awarded the high Order of the Black Eagle by Emperor Wilhelm I; Prince Ludwig hurried to Berlin around mid-January 1872 to be invested with the aforementioned order on the occasion of the Prussian coronation anniversary and order celebration (*Krönungs- und*

---

[64] Grand Duke Ernst Ludwig wrote that his father had expressed a prophetic warning: *I remember that he was very worried around the year 1890, because he said that the German army and the German people were too warlike, and that especially the officer corps looked down too much on the French and the English 'because they had nothing of the military spirit'. That would be quite wrong. In 1870, he had seen that despite their poor leadership, the French had done well and the Englishman would always be tenacious in his pursuits, which he had already proved too often. If there were a war, in particular with the French, we would be very surprised at how good they were, and we would not find it easy to defeat them.* (Ernst Ludwig Grossherzog von Hessen und bei Rhein, *Erinnertes*, 46)

Ordensfest). In the beginning of the same year, he went to Metz with his wife, Princess Alice, and attended the inauguration of the beautiful monument of a bronze lion on the battlefield of the Hessian division at the Bois de la Cusse in honour of the soldiers who had fallen and were buried there.[65] Prince Ludwig of Hesse himself spoke a few words of comradely remembrance that came from the depth of his heart and concluded with a cheer for Emperor Wilhelm I and Grand Duke Ludwig III.

In 1873, Prince Ludwig was given some joyful news. On Sedan Day, 2 September 1873, Emperor Wilhelm placed him as a lieutenant general à la suite at the disposal of the 1st Foot Guard Regiment; thus, he saw himself once again closely associated with the same regiment in the ranks of which he had served for several years as a young prince during his military training. Towards the end of the year, he visited the English royal court in Windsor and London with his wife and some of his family, and the family reunited in Darmstadt for Christmas.

The year 1874 also passed in external peace and was filled with diligent work. The prince visited the seaside resort of Blankenberghe again with his family in the months of July and August. On 16 August, the prince had the opportunity to save a lady from drowning there, placing his own life in danger to do so. His wife left the following interesting record of this event: *'Yesterday Louis saved a lady from drowning. He was bathing. The waves were high, and he heard a cry for help, and saw a bather struggling. She had lost her footing. Her husband tried to help her, but was exhausted*

---

[65] The Bois de la Cusse was a small patch of forest between the villages of Amanvillers and Habonville, a few kilometers west of the city of Metz. The fight at the Bois de la Cusse was part of the Battle of Gravelotte-St. Privat (i.e., Saint-Privat-la-Montagne) on 18 August 1870.

It appears that Zernin is mistaken here. The monument was not inaugurated at the beginning but at the end of that year – on 9 November 1872. See Alice Grand Duchess of Hesse, *Alice*, 297, and the description of the inauguration in *Darmstädter Zeitung*, 14 November 1872.

and let her go; equally so the brother-in-law, and Louis felt he was losing his strength, but she kept her presence of mind and floated. He let her go once till a wave brought her near him again, and he caught her hand and brought her in, feeling quite done himself. (…) The lady is a Mrs J. Sligo, a Scotchwoman, and she has just written to me to thank Louis. He is a good swimmer, and very strong.'[66]

The imperial manoeuvre (*Kaisermanöver*) of the 11th Army Corps followed in September 1874. It was held in Upper Hesse before Emperor Wilhelm I. The Grand-ducal Hessian (25th) Division again had to prove its quality at this manoeuvre. Emperor Wilhelm I, the strict and incorruptible judge of all military achievements, found no reason for dismissals; he gladly took every opportunity to widely praise the achievements of the Hessian troops during the first major manoeuvre days and, in particular, to express his sincere appreciation to its capable leader for everything he observed in him.

---

[66] [Note by G. Zernin:] Alice Grand Duchess of Hesse, *Alice*, 331.

Sovereign (1877–1892)

The year 1877 brought about a major change. First, Prince Ludwig's father, Prince Carl of Hesse, who was not yet 68 years of age, fell ill with erysipelas on the night of 11 March; the infection took his life on 20 March. Several weeks later, Grand Duke Ludwig III also fell seriously ill at his summer residence, Seeheim, and closed his eyes forever at half past ten in the morning of 13 June, a few days after he had attained the age of 71. The heir to the throne was Prince Ludwig, who, according to a decree passed on 13 June, took over the government as Grand Duke Ludwig IV. The new Grand Duke resigned the command of the Grand-ducal Hessian (25th) Division on 29 June and issued the following divisional order:

Having today relinquished the command of the Division, I feel compelled to express my warmest and heartfelt thanks to all the members of this Division for the trust shown to me in war and peace during the eleven years I had the honour of commanding the Division, for the joyful obedience, the discipline of men and the active, zealous service. The decoration for 25 years of service that I have just been awarded will always remind me of the many comrades and loyal subordinates, who I am convinced will keep as good a memory of their retiring superior as their present warlord keeps of them.

Ludwig of Hesse, Lieutenant General

The high-born gentleman celebrated his fortieth birthday on 12 September 1877, this time as Grand Duke of Hesse and by Rhine. On the same day, he took over the position of Colonel-in-Chief of the 1st Grand-ducal Hessian Infantry (Lifeguards) Regiment No. 115, of the 1st Grand-ducal Hessian Dragoon Regiment (Guard Dragoon Regiment) No. 23, and of the Grand-ducal Hessian Field Artillery Regiment (Grand-ducal Artillery Corps) No. 25. Shortly before this, on 23 June 1877, His Majesty King Ludwig II of Bavaria had granted the 5th Royal Bavarian

Infantry Regiment to Grand Duke Ludwig IV, which had become available by the death of Grand Duke Ludwig III and which was already established in 1722 and comes with a rich history.

However, Emperor Franz Joseph of Austria also wished to see the name of the Grand Duke of Hesse preserved in his brave army and granted the Imperial and Royal Infantry Regiment No. 14, which was garrisoned in Linz on the Danube, to Grand Duke Ludwig IV of Hesse on 9 December 1877. The Emperor's cabinet letter is so indicative of the good reputation of the Hessian name that it deserves to be reproduced here:

Most Serene and dear cousin and Grand Duke!

Since the sad passing away of the most serene uncle of Your Royal Highness, my Line Regiment No. 14, which carries the name of the immortalized, has not been appointed to a colonel-in-chief again. It is the memory of old and proven ties that connect me and my House with the illustrious lineage to which Your Royal Highness belongs that makes me wish to preserve the name for an excellent regiment which has earned such high claims to my recognition under this name. The said regiment will only see in this a new incentive to strictly fulfil the duties it owes to this name. I therefore feel determined to appoint Your Royal Highness as colonel-in-chief of my 14th Line Infantry Regiment. In hoping that Your Royal Highness will see in this appointment a proof of the warm and sincere sentiments which I have always had for the Grand-ducal House of Hesse, I remain in perfect esteem.

Your Royal Highness's benevolent cousin Franz Joseph.

Vienna, 9 December 1877

All these high and deserved honours delighted the Grand Duke very much, but they were not able to alleviate the heavy weight on his heart due to the illness of his wife, the Grand Duchess Alice, which was developing at that time. Alice was not able to accompany her husband to the double wedding of the Hohenzollern Princess Charlotte of Prussia with the Hereditary

Prince of Meiningen and of Princess Elisabeth of Prussia with the Hereditary Grand Duke of Oldenburg, which took place at Berlin Palace (*Berliner Schloss*) on 18 February 1878.[67] Not even a visit to the seaside resort of Eastbourne near Hastings in the summer of 1878 could improve the health of the Grand Duke's wife in the long term. In November of the same year, the Grand-ducal family in Darmstadt was struck by the treacherous disease of diphtheria. The disease claimed the life of the little four-year-old Princess Marie on 16 November. Her noble mother also passed away a few weeks later, on 14 December, after she had fallen seriously ill with the same disease a week earlier; it was assumed that she had absorbed the contagious matter when she once bowed her head onto the pillow of her husband, who was also ill, in pain over their lost child. Now the Grand Duke stood alone as a widower with his five surviving children; however, he fought his sorrow in a manly manner and vowed to compensate his family and his country for the loss of its mother and grand duchess through double loyalty to duty as far as possible. Conscientiously, he followed this vow until the end of his own life. On 11 June 1879, His Majesty Emperor Wilhelm I promoted him to general of the infantry. The emperor showed his personal joy about this promotion by adding the following words to the telegram of appointment:

I am particularly pleased to inform Your Royal Highness of this, remaining with sincere esteem and friendship
          Your Royal Highness's
                 friendly cousin and brother, Wilhelm.

---

[67] Princess Charlotte of Prussia (1860–1919) was the first daughter of Friedrich III of Prussia (1831–1888) and, therefore, a sister of Wilhelm II. She married Bernard, the Hereditary Duke of Saxe-Meiningen (1851–1928), who came to the throne only in 1914.

    Princess Elisabeth Anne of Prussia (1857–1895) was the second daughter of Prince Friedrich Karl of Prussia (1828–1885), whose father was Prince Carl of Prussia (1801–1883), Wilhelm I's brother. She married Prince Friedrich August of Oldenburg (1852–1931), the Hereditary Grand Duke of Oldenburg.

Until the end of his long and richly blessed life, the supreme commander had no more faithful and zealous helper in the training of the German army than Grand Duke Ludwig IV of Hesse and by Rhine. The Grand Duke's main inclinations remained military, although as a sovereign, the high-born gentleman had to direct his attention and efforts to numerous other aspects; he conscientiously endeavoured to fulfil his numerous obligations. Soon after his accession to the throne, Emperor Friedrich III also honoured him by appointing him Inspector General of the 3rd Army Inspectorate in recognition of his proven care. This appointment took place on a beautiful family day for the Hessian and Prussian courts – 24 May 1888 – when the hands of Prince Heinrich of Prussia and Princess Irene of Hesse were joined for the covenant of life at Charlottenburg Palace (*Schloss Charlottenburg*).[68]

Grand Duke Ludwig IV was active in his capacity as General Inspector of the 3rd Army Inspectorate for almost four years. As such, he had to supervise the military training of the 7th, 8th, and 11th Army Corps – that is, a total of seven divisions – inspect them personally, and to strive for their perfection. He took this difficult task seriously and had the great pleasure of seeing his efforts recognized, particularly by Emperor Wilhelm II, as has been publicly stated several times by the same sovereign. In particular, this happened on the occasion of the large imperial manoeuvres, conducted by the 11th Army Corps near Kassel in September 1891, during which Grand Duke Ludwig IV acted as inspector general. The parade of this army corps, which took place on 12 September was attended by a large number of royals, such as the King of

---

[68] Prince Heinrich of Prussia (1862–1929) was the second son of the then reigning German Emperor Friedrich III; Princess Irene of Hesse and by Rhine (1866–1953) was the third daughter of Grand Duke Ludwig IV. Friedrich III was the German Emperor since 9 March 1888, but would die on 15 June of that same year. The location of the wedding, the baroque Charlottenburg Palace, is situated in the Charlottenburg quarter of Berlin.

Saxony, the Grand Dukes of Hesse and Saxe-Weimar, the Princes Heinrich and Albrecht of Prussia, the Duke of Edinburgh, and the Princesses Heinrich of Prussia and Alix of Hesse on horseback.[69] At the parade dinner at the City Palace (*Stadtschloss*),[70] the Emperor made a toast to the 11th Army Corps, which was introduced by the following words:

I begin my toast to the welfare of the 11th Army Corps by expressing my heartfelt thanks to all my illustrious cousins for coming here to parade at the head of their regiments and, thus, to give it a more celebratory character.

A special distinction for Grand Duke Ludwig IV was also found in the fact that he was promoted by the supreme commander, Emperor Wilhelm II, to colonel general of the infantry with the rank of field marshal general on the same day – his 54th birthday. This was done through the following handwritten personal message:

To the Grand Duke of Hesse and by Rhine Royal Highness, General of the Infantry and Inspector General of the 3rd Army Inspectorate.

Most Serene Sovereign,
dear cousin, brother and uncle!
This day and the presence of Your Royal Highness at the manoeuvres gives me the desired occasion to give Your Royal Highness a sign of my

---

[69] King Albert of Saxony (1828–1902), Grand Duke Ludwig IV of Hesse and by Rhine (1837–1892), Grand Duke Karl Alexander of Saxe-Weimar-Eisenach (1818–1901), Prince Heinrich of Prussia (1862–1929) and Prince Albrecht of Prussia (1837–1906), Princess Heinrich of Prussia, née Princess Irene of Hesse (1866–1953), and Princess Alix of Hesse (1872–1918).

[70] The City Palace referred to was presumably the Residential Palace in the city of Kassel – that is, the complex of the former White Palace (*Weisses Palais*) and Red Palace (*Rotes Palais*) on Friedrichsplatz in Kassel, situated next to the Fridericianum museum. Both the White Palace and the Red Palace were destroyed during World War II. See also *Darmstädter Zeitung* dated 14 September 1891.

special esteem and affection by promoting you to colonel general of the Infantry with the rank of field marshal general. I remain, with sentiments of unchanging friendship

> Your Royal Highness's
>> friendly cousin, brother, and nephew, Wilhelm.
>>> Schloss Wilhelmshöhe, 12 September 1891

Highly pleased and driven by the desire to show his gratitude for the honour bestowed upon him, the Grand Duke asked Emperor Wilhelm II to take over the position of colonel-in-chief of the 2nd Grand-ducal Hessian Infantry Regiment No. 116 'Grand Duke'. His Majesty gladly fulfilled this wish and, thus, Grand Duke Ludwig IV issued the following order of the day on the very next day:

>> Kassel, 13 September 1891

Yesterday, His Majesty the Emperor had the grace to take over the position of colonel-in-chief of the 2nd Infantry Regiment No. 116.

This is a distinction which, together with my most gracious appointment as colonel general of the infantry, must fill the division with pride and joy. It has earned the satisfaction of the supreme commander, and I am sure that the regiment will do honour to its new name 'Kaiser' as it has done to its name 'Grand Duke' until now, and will continue to do so in the future, on all occasions, in war and in peace.

>> signed Ludwig,
>> Colonel General

Now, Grand Duke Ludwig IV of Hesse and by Rhine had achieved the highest military rank. He saw his long years of work in war and peace splendidly acknowledged by the supreme commander and, thus, he must have been satisfied with his own achievements. However, in line with his innermost nature, he remained as modest as he was earlier and faithfully performed all duties and obligations incumbent upon him as inspector general and colonel general of the infantry and as sovereign and first servant of his country.[71]

---

[71] In her biography of Grand Duke Ludwig's daughter Alix, Sophie Buxhoeveden wrote the following lines: '*He took his duties as ruler seriously, and was interested in politics outside his little Grand Duchy. He hailed the idea of a United Germany, though Hesse had lost so much territory to Prussia.*' (Sophie Buxhoeveden, *The Life and Tragedy of Alexandra Feodorovna Empress of Russia: A Biography* (London: Longmans, Green, 1930), 28)

Manfred Knodt, the biographer of Grand Duke Ludwig's son Ernst Ludwig, provided the following details: *It was (…) Ludwig IV who carried out the reorientation of Hesse towards Prussia, whereby he, the son-in-law of Queen Victoria, admittedly had other political ideas in mind for the German Empire than those later realized by Wilhelm II, the eldest grandson of the Queen. By marrying Princess Alice of the United Kingdom, Ludwig IV did not give Hesse (…) political world significance, but a world opening, one might say in modern terms, a European consciousness.* (Manfred Knodt, *Ernst Ludwig Grossherzog von Hessen und bei Rhein: Sein Leben und Seine Zeit,* 2nd ed. (Darmstadt: Schlapp, 1985), 57)

Moreover, shortly after the death of Grand Duke Ludwig IV in 1892, his daughter Victoria wrote the following remembrance: '*He was one of the kindest-hearted and most just men I have ever known. He was as liberal as he was fair-minded and did not approve of Bismarck's "socialist laws". My father understood his people well and they him. To give an instance of this, when he drove himself home from a long day's shoot through very socialistically minded villages, the peasants, on hearing the tramp of his Hungarian "Jucker" team, would put their lamps in the window sills to lighten up the streets.*' (Victoria Marchioness of Milford Haven, *Recollections,* 74 of the PDF file)

Last illness and death (1892)

Since his return from the imperial manoeuvres in 1891, the Grand Duke no longer appeared as vigorous as he had almost always been. In those days, he often said that he felt he would probably not live much longer. His entourage was always highly surprised by such outbursts, for the Grand Duke continued to look healthy. Unfortunately, his dismal words were to come true only too quickly. On 6 November 1891, on the day after the 25th anniversary celebration of the 1st Hessian Infantry Regiment No. 81 – of which the Grand Duke had been commander since 1871 – and on which occasion he had enjoyed the very friendly and companionable company of the officers and men of his Prussian regiment, he paid a visit to the Prince of Leiningen.[72] During this visit, the Grand Duke had great difficulty breathing when he ascended a steep hill, which was the first sure sign of a serious illness developing. On the advice of the Grand Duke's personal physician, Privy Councillor Dr Eigenbrodt, Professor Kussmaul from Heidelberg was sent for a few days later.[73] On 4 March 1892, at 3 pm, Grand Duke Ludwig IV was struck by a stroke. The right half of his body was paralyzed, but he was still conscious. On 6 March, personal physicians Dr Eigenbrodt and Dr Jäger[74] as well as Professor Kussmaul announced that the Grand Duke was still unable to speak, but that his general strength was not affected. However, he lost consciousness on 8 March. After an

---

[72] Ernst (1830–1904), the 4th Prince of Leiningen, was a member of the upper chamber of the parliament of the Grand Duchy of Hesse and by Rhine.

[73] Professor Adolf Kussmaul (1822–1902) was a German internist and gastroenterologist. Dr Karl Eigenbrodt (1826–1900) had been the personal physician of Grand Duke Ludwig IV and his family since 1877. Dr Eigenbrodt was promoted from *Geheimer Medizinalrat* to *Geheimerat* on 26 March 1892.

[74] Dr Wilhelm Jäger (1839–1910) was a first lieutenant and medical officer of health (*Medizinalrat*) in Darmstadt. Dr Jäger was promoted to *Geheimer Medizinalrat* on 26 March 1892.

apparently brief improvement, Grand Duke Ludwig IV gently passed away to a better life at the age of 54.5 years at half past one on the morning of 13 March.

Character sketch and conclusion

Grand Duke Ludwig IV had an unwavering loyalty to duty. He not only listened to the appointed councillors of the crown who were close to him but also lent an ear to each individual subject and received all people from all classes who had special wishes or requests to present. Numerous individual cases have come to light in which Ludwig IV himself, in response to brief allusions in the daily press, took the opportunity to investigate complaints and grievances and attempted to remedy them.

It has become generally known that the Grand Duke was always characterized by the greatest federal loyalty to the head of the German Empire, the supreme commander of the German army. Moreover, as sovereign, he submitted himself gladly and undauntedly to all that was required of him to ensure the welfare of his three provinces[75] and took pride in correctly recognizing and satisfying the needs of these rather differently shaped parts of the country on both banks of the River Rhine and north of the River Main.

The Grand Duke distinguished himself by excellent qualities of heart and mind. His main virtues were simplicity, conscientiousness, moral uprightness, and natural benevolence.[76]

---

[75] The Grand Duchy of Hesse was divided into the provinces of Upper Hesse (*Oberhessen*), Rhine-Hesse (*Rheinhessen*), and Starkenburg.

[76] Ernst Ludwig, Grand Duke Ludwig IV's son, provided a few examples of his father's benevolence and simplicity in his memoirs:

He almost always drove a four-in-hand by himself. Coming back from a hunt one day, he was in a great hurry because he still had to receive people. There he came across a poor country woman dragging a load of wood by herself, alone in the forest. He stopped and asked her where she was going. It was to the next village, but not in his direction. The woman was quickly put behind him in the carriage and the coachmen had to hold the load of wood in their arms. Now he set off, and hurried all the way to the village at a gallop, set down the woman and her wood, chased back on his way, and still arrived in Darmstadt in time. Another time, also returning from a hunt, he was riding in a heavy snowstorm. There he met an old postman struggling against the

In addition, the Grand Duke was a soldier before all else – a soldier from top to toe, who proved his worth in war and peace and who used his rich military experience and knowledge in the interest of the domestic military power. He was also an affable and philanthropic man who knew how to win over not only officers but also ordinary people.[77]

We dedicate a special section to the troop commander Prince Ludwig of Hesse in the Franco-Prussian War of 1870–1871 here, based on the information given about him by two participants in this campaign. The first is the well-known military writer Captain Fritz Hoenig,[78] who made the following observations:

... At the head of the division was Prince Ludwig of Hesse. The prince was 33 years old at that time; he was of medium height, possessed great physical strength, had been hardened from youth and thus, immune to weather influences, and enjoyed a robust health. He had no consideration for himself; he expected his body to make the greatest efforts without ever complaining of fatigue and he was always active. The prince had a

---

storm. He quickly stopped; the postman had to get in; he turned around and drove him back to where the man was going, dropped him off, turned around again and drove on home. He was like that, and no one knew anything about it, because his people had strict orders to keep quiet. How many times did he perform such labours of love? I know these two stories through Germann, who had been his and my bodyguard, but only many years after his death. (Ernst Ludwig Grossherzog von Hessen und bei Rhein, *Erinnertes*, 46–47)

The 'bodyguard' was presumably *Hofjäger* Daniel German (1847–1922), gamekeeper.

[77] According to Ernst Ludwig, Grand Duke Ludwig IV was also a man who, occasionally, would find it difficult to make a decision in order not to hurt anyone. Ernst Ludwig recognised that avoiding unpleasant discussions for the sake of peace was unfortunately a drawback of the family. (Ernst Ludwig Grossherzog von Hessen und bei Rhein, *Erinnertes*, 44)

[78] Frits Hoenig (1804–1922) was an officer in the infantry and a military writer. He took part in the Austro-Prussian War in 1866 as well as in the Franco-German War in 1870–1871. He was wounded in the first battle fought by the Hessian division in the latter war, the Battle of Vionville-Mars-la-Tour on 16 August 1870.

friendly, engaging nature, he was always helpful, and extremely modest.[79] *He was also very energetic and always reliable. He exuded extraordinary physical and moral courage, but he did not like it when someone mentioned it or even praised him for it, because he thought that this was a natural quality of every soldier. On the other hand, every courageous act of a subordinate filled him with great joy, and he liked to talk about it with appreciation, especially when determination and courage to accept responsibility were evident.*

The prince was a soldier in heart and soul,[80] *a good and bold horseman and a passionate hunter; he shared these inclinations with Prince Friedrich Karl of Prussia.*[81] *He developed a similar activity in the Hessian army division after the unfortunate year of 1866, as Prince Friedrich Karl had done in the Prussian army. The prince was a special admirer of the Prussian army; it was his example. This admiration originated not only from to the Prussian successes in 1864 and 1866 but also from the accurate knowledge the prince had of the Prussian army. However, the prince was also very well informed about the conditions in the other foreign armies, especially about the infantry and its tactics; he was even fully aware of details. He was one of those who had urged the conclusion of the first convention with Prussia, although he did not entirely approve of its execution.*[82]

---

[79] Grand Duke Ernst Ludwig on his father's modesty: *He had a great modesty, so that through him none of us had the so-called princely conceit, because every person was equal to us. This also meant that we were modest towards humanity and often did not appear as firm as was necessary.* (Ernst Ludwig Grossherzog von Hessen und bei Rhein, *Erinnertes*, 46)

[80] Ernst Ludwig confirmed, *My father was a soldier in heart and soul, but not so-called 'military' in the true, great sense. He never let trivialities, of which there are so many necessary in the service, dominate him. Veteran officers from 1866 and 1870–1871 have told me that he was the bravest man they knew. He did not know what fear was, but he was never foolhardy. (…) He once said to me, 'Anyone who has participated in a war as an able soldier and later speaks in favour of war should be hanged.'* (Ernst Ludwig Grossherzog von Hessen und bei Rhein, *Erinnertes*, 46)

[81] Prince Friedrich Karl of Prussia (1828–1885).

[82] [Note by G. Zernin:] As is well-known, this first military convention was

The prince possessed an amazing sense of orientation and would read maps with the greatest speed. The prince also possessed other qualities that so often result from hunting and warfare: simplicity, undemandingness, camaraderie, and affability. As a true hunter, he could get up at any time of the night, which should not be undervalued in a leader. He maintained a loyal disposition towards everyone with whom he had come into contact.

The prince was a cautious and determined leader. But he also knew exactly the needs of the soldiers and knew how to take and treat young people excellently. There was one thing that struck his entourage in this war: the toughness that he showed on himself he did not apply to the generals under him, who were much older in years. This is difficult in itself; in this case it is also explained by the fact that higher positions in the Hessian division were often occupied by Prussian officers, whose abilities the prince had great respect for. The officers and soldiers revered the prince; they had great confidence in him, always ready to take responsibility for the actions of his subordinates. The patriotic spirit of the prince is of particular importance for history. Anyone who knows more about the circumstances of the time will think very highly of it. And since the war, the Prince, and later Grand Duke, remained an enthusiastic sympathizer of what had been achieved. His speeches and decrees came from the heart and went to the heart; he took pride in having been the leader of his Hessians in the German Unification war, and it must be gratefully acknowledged that the prince also took a warm interest in war history and promoted it to the best of his ability. The descriptions of the war of 1870–1871 by Hessian officers are among the best in the literature; we only need to recall the work of Scherf-Draudt.[83]

The assessment by Hoenig reproduced here corresponds exactly with our own views as well as with those of other Hessian

---

agreed in 1867 and was replaced by the 1872 military convention.

[83] [Note by G. Zernin:] Cf. *Der Volkskrieg an der Loire im Herbst 1870, 5. Band; die entscheidenden Tage von Orléans im Herbst 1870, 3. Theil: die Auflösung des französischen Heeres vor Orléans (der 3. Dezember 1870). Mit 3 Kartenbeilagen* (Berlin: E. S. Mittler & Sohn, 1897), 121 et seq.

officers. To prove this, let us see what the now deceased Grand-ducal staff officer Lieutenant Colonel Ferdinand von Hessert[84] once wrote on the same subject. He wrote the following in the Introduction to a short document:

At the head of the Hessian division was Prince Ludwig, who is now (1879) our Grand Duke. Prince Ludwig had entered the Hessian service at the same time as his brother Prince Heinrich. As lieutenants, both princes performed the same duties as any other officer; at all times, in the heat and the cold, one could see the youthful brothers present. Later, both princes joined the Royal Prussian Army. There, Prince Ludwig got to know the course of duty and training in the Guards Corps, which is imitated by almost all armies in the world today.

Prince Ludwig took command of the Hessian division immediately after the campaign of 1866, directed its training according to the rules of Prussian service and practice, and experienced the joy of being able to lead his Hessians across the Rhine to safeguard the freedom of his fatherland, just as his great uncle Prince Emil of Hesse,[85] who was highly esteemed in the memory of the veterans of the campaigns of 1814 and 1815, had done in the past.[86]

Until shortly before his death, Grand Duke Ludwig IV enjoyed good, lasting health of which his blooming appearance was the best proof. Educated in a fairly harsh manner, the prince was always a supporter of all strengthening physical exercises and knightly games: a capable horseman and fencer, a skilful dancer and skater, a good swimmer and oarsman, and also an excellent

---

[84] Ferdinand von Hessert was an officer who served as a captain in the Hessian infantry during the Austro-Prussian War of 1866 and, by then having the rank of major, as commander of the 2nd battalion of the 3rd Infantry Regiment in the Franco-German War of 1870–1871.

[85] Prince Emil of Hesse and by Rhine (1790–1856), the fourth son of Grand Duke Ludwig I of Hesse, had fought as a commander in the Napoleonic Wars.

[86] [Note by G. Zernin:] Cf.: *Die Hessen in der Schlacht bei Gravelotte-St. Privat, ein Gedenkblatt zur Enthüllungsfeier des Landes-Krieger-Denkmals am 18. August 1879* (Darmstadt and Leipzig, 1879).

driver of a four-in-hand. The Grand Duke's main passion – the same as of many of his Hessian ancestors – was the noble sport of hunting; the number of rare prey animals which his sure hand bagged on the most diverse hunting grounds of Europe is extraordinarily large. A beautifully arranged selection of antlers of all kinds is displayed in the old Kranichstein hunting lodge near Darmstadt and delights the eye and heart of every true huntsman.

At our request, a close acquaintance of the Grand Duke – a close relative of his who grew up with him from childhood – provided us with an assessment of Grand Duke Ludwig IV's character for this publication. In short, it is aptly summarized below:

A lively, cheerful temperament, unselfish, genuine, striving to be fair to everyone, an enemy of all flattery and hypocrisy, a practical nature, a friend of all sports, a true hunter, a passionate soldier, undemanding for his person, not a friend of luxury.

* * *

Thus, the image of the radiant sovereign lives on in the memory of his immediate circle, and so it will also live on in the grateful memory of his loyal soldiers and subjects.

Grand Duke Ludwig IV and his family, 1877
(©Staatsarchiv Darmstadt, R 4 Nr. 25425)

Prince Ludwig of Hesse and by Rhine in 1875,
before he became Grand Duke Ludwig IV
(© Großherzogliches Familienarchiv im Staatsarchiv Darmstadt,
D 27 A Nr. 48/280)

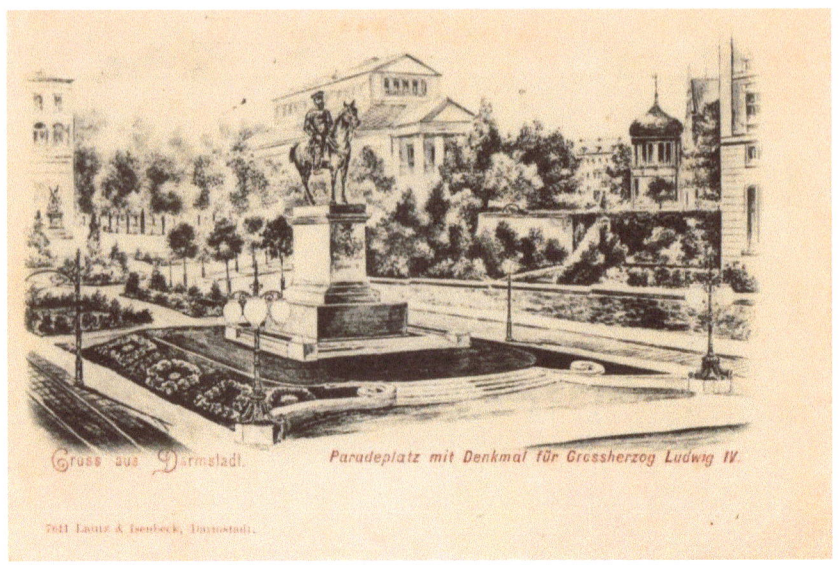

The equestrian statue of Ludwig IV on Paradeplatz in Darmstadt (Author's collection)

The equestrian statue of Grand Duke Ludwig IV on the day of its unveiling (© Staatsarchiv Darmstadt, R 4 Nr. 30947)

The monument for the Hessian soldiers fallen on the battlefield at the Bois de la Cusse (Author's collection)

The war monument for the miliary men from Hesse fallen in the 1870–1871 Franco-German war on Paradeplatz in Darmstadt. This monument was taken down in 1952. (Author's collection)

The equestrian statue of Ludwig IV on Paradeplatz in Darmstadt
(Author's collection)

The unveiling of the equestrian statue in Darmstadt (1898)

Shortly after the death of Grand Duke Ludwig IV, the idea arose to honour him with a statue in Darmstadt, the capital of the Grand Duchy. A monument committee was established, headed by Bruno, Prince of Ysenburg and Büdingen (1837–1906), president of the Hessian upper chamber.[87] Funds for the establishment of the monument were raised from organisations as well as from monetary donations by numerous people from all walks of life. The committee decided that an equestrian statue must be erected. The statue would depict Ludwig IV as commanding officer of the Hessian division in the Franco-Prussian War of 1870–1871. It was designed by Fritz Schaper and cast out of iron by brothers Walter and Paul Gladenbeck.[88] The location selected for the statue was next to the Residential Palace on Paradeplatz.

The foundation stone of the statue was laid on 21 September 1898.[89] Architect Müller and Prince Bruno of Ysenburg and Büdingen addressed a select group of invitees, and *Geheimer Regierungsrat* Haas read aloud a calligraphic document, which was then placed in a copper container in the foundation stone.[90] The unveiling of the statue took place on Friday 25 November 1898, which was also the birthday of the reigning Grand Duke Ernst Ludwig of Hesse and by Rhine and of his wife, Grand Duchess Victoria Melita. A detailed account of the unveiling was printed in the morning edition of the *Darmstädter Zeitung* newspaper dated 26 November 1898 under the headline 'Die Enthüllung des

---

[87] *Darmstädter Zeitung*, 26 November 1898, morning edition.
[88] Mona Sauer, 'Reiterdenkmal', Stadtlexikon Darmstadt (Historischer Verein für Hessen e. V.), accessed 6 January 2023.
https://www.darmstadt-stadtlexikon.de/r/reiterdenkmal.html.
[89] *Darmstädter Zeitung*, 21 September 1898, afternoon edition.
[90] Heinrich Müller (1849–1906), Wilhelm Haas (1839–1913).

Reiterdenkmals', with further information in the afternoon edition of 26 November as well as the editions of preceding and subsequent days. This newspaper also carried advertisements for Gebhard Zernin's biographical sketch of Grand Duke Ludwig IV, copies of which could be obtained for 50 pfennigs, as well as for postcards with images of the equestrian statue.

Ludwig IV's eldest daughter, Victoria, who was married to Prince Ludwig of Battenberg, remembered that '... *on Ernie's birthday, November 25th, we were all present at the unveiling of Papa's equestrian statue on the so-called "Paradeplatz"* ....'[91] It is true that Victoria attended the festivities and that her sister Elisabeth and her husband Grand Duke Sergei Alexandrovich of Russia were also present. Grand Duke Sergei Alexandrovich and Grand Duchess Elisabeth arrived from Windsor in Darmstadt on 24 November.[92] However, unfortunately, Ludwig IV's daughters Irene and Alix could not attend the actual unveiling.

The reason for Princess Irene's absence was evident: on the day of the unveiling, she was on her way to visit her husband – Prince Heinrich of Prussia – in Kiao-Chau, China. However, she came to Darmstadt before her departure for China, arriving by train on the morning of Saturday 12 November 1898. She went to see her father's equestrian statue along with her sister Princess Victoria, *Oberhofmarschall* Paul Westerweller von Anthoni (1827–1912), and Lieutenant General Paul Wernher (1839–1901) on Monday 14 November. They met with *Geheimer Regierungsrat* Haas and architect Müller at the location of the statue. According to *Darmstädter Zeitung*, Victoria and Irene were visibly moved and expressed their satisfaction with the statue.[93] As Princess Victoria noted in her memoirs, the equestrian statue on Paradeplatz was '*a*

---

[91] Victoria Marchioness of Milford Haven, *Recollections*, 98 of the PDF file.
[92] *Darmstädter Zeitung*, 24 November 1898, afternoon edition.
[93] *Darmstädter Zeitung*, 22 November 1898, afternoon edition.

simple and, therefore, characteristic representation of him in his ordinary military undress'.⁹⁴ On the evening of that Monday, Irene said her farewells and departed for Italy, where she boarded the Lloyd Steamship called 'Prinz Heinrich' to Kiao-Chau.

Grand Duke Ludwig IV's daughter Alix, who was married to Emperor Nicholas II of Russia, was not present at the actual unveiling either. She was staying with her husband and their two daughters in Livadia in Crimea. The Empress's letters to Grand Duke Ernst Ludwig do not provide any information regarding the reason for her absence. The imperial couple may not have had any plans to come to Darmstadt, but it is also possible that they cancelled any such plans during November. One possible reason for their absence could be the fact that Emperor Nicholas II had to be back in Crimea by 30 November to attend the unveiling of a monument for Admiral Pavel Stepanovich Nakhimov (1802–1855) who had fought in the Battle of Sinope on 30 November 1853 and the defence of Sebastopol during the Crimean War.⁹⁵ Another possible reason why Tsar Nicholas and his wife may have preferred to stay in Livadia is the fact that Nicholas had already travelled abroad, unexpectedly, for over two weeks in October to attend the memorial services for and interment of his maternal grandmother, the Queen Consort of Denmark, *née* Princess Louise of Hesse-Kassel (1817–1898), in Roskilde Cathedral near Copenhagen.⁹⁶ An additional reason may have been that the

---

[94] Victoria Marchioness of Milford Haven, *Recollections*, 98 of the PDF file.

[95] *Darmstädter Zeitung*, 10 November 1898, morning edition. See also Tsar Nicholas II's diary entries for 17–18 November 1898 (Julian calendar dates). Nicholas II, *Dnevniki Imperatora Nikolaja II (1894–1918): 1894–1904*, ed. Sergei Vladimirovich Mironenko, (Moscow: Rosspen, 2011), 444; Nicholas II, *The Diaries of Nicholas II, 1897–1900*, translated, edited and annotated by Stephen R. de Angelis, (USA: Bookemon, 2014), 153–154.

[96] Tsar Nicholas II's diary entries for 17 September to 9 October 1898 (Julian calendar dates). Nicholas II, *Dnevniki Imperatora Nikolaja II (1894–1918): 1894–1904*, 433–437; Nicholas II, *The Diaries of Nicholas II, 1897–1900*, 142–147.

Empress was pregnant with her third child and was *'not feeling especially well'*. Nicholas remarked in his diary: *'It is all strongly wiping her out.'* [97] Their daughter Maria was born on 26 June 1899 (14 June 1899 in the Julian calendar).

In the days leading up to the celebrations, other relatives of Ludwig IV also came to Darmstadt. The Duke of Saxe-Coburg and Gotha, Grand Duchess Victoria Melita's father, arrived in Darmstadt as early as Sunday 20 November. The duke seized the opportunity to go hunting for wild boars in Kranichstein park on Monday 21 November and to go hunting with Major von Heijl near the village of Pfeddersheim, today a borough of Worms, on Tuesday 22 November. Ludwig IV's brother Prince Heinrich of Hesse arrived on 22 November.[98] Emperor Wilhelm II could not attend the unveiling, as he and his wife were on their way home after a state visit to the Levant. He was represented by Prince Friedrich Leopold of Prussia, who arrived in Darmstadt in the morning of 25 November.[99]

The unveiling of the statue stirred enormous interest among the people of Hesse. Delegations from various official bodies and associations as well as private individuals came from all parts of the Grand Duchy to Darmstadt in the days leading up to the celebrations. To make the journey to Darmstadt more affordable for such people, the operators of certain railway lines to Darmstadt, including the Rhein-Neckarbahn, offered discounts on the price of train tickets for regional trains – people who had bought a single ticket to Darmstadt could travel back home on the same ticket for free.

---

[97] Tsar Nicholas II's diary entries for 19 October 1898 and 11 November 1898 (Julian calendar dates). Nicholas II, *Dnevniki Imperatora Nikolaja II (1894–1918): 1894–1904*, 439 and 443; Nicholas II, *The Diaries of Nicholas II, 1897–1900*, 149 and 152.
[98] *Darmstädter Zeitung*, 19 November 1898, afternoon edition.
[99] *Darmstädter Zeitung*, 26 November 1898, afternoon edition.

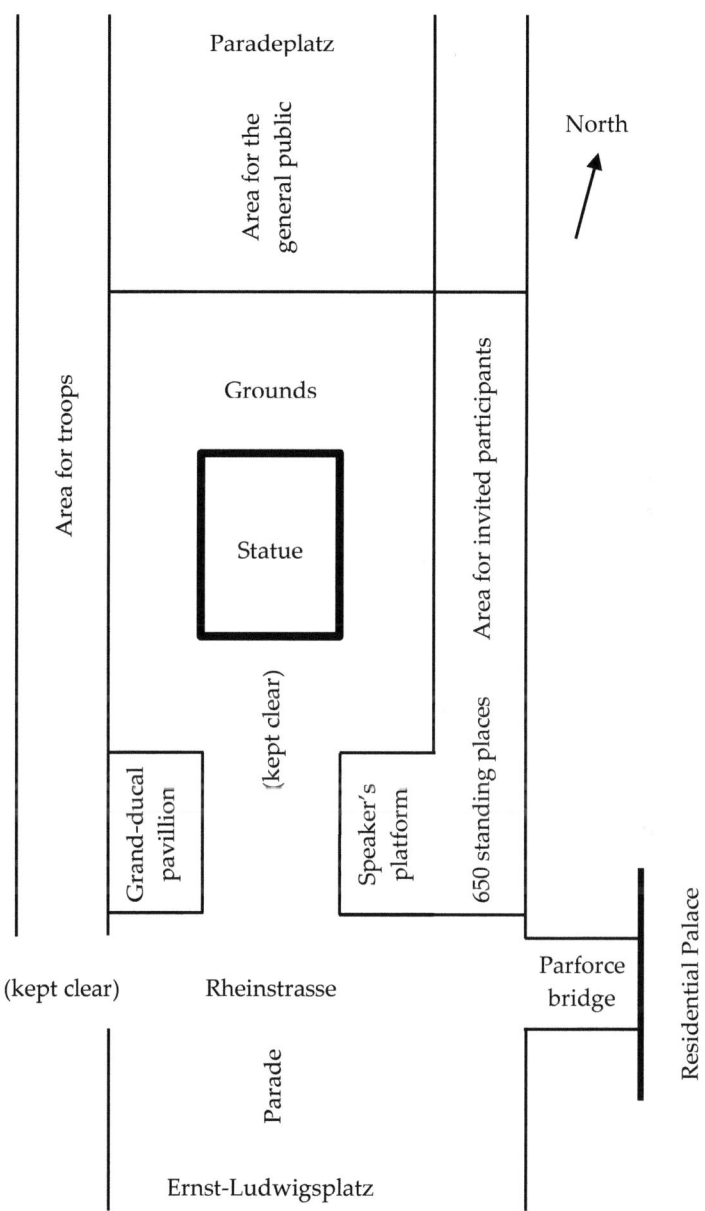

Initial layout of Paradeplatz on 25 November 1898 as published in the afternoon edition of *Darmstädter Zeitung* of 12 November 1898.

Among the people who came to Darmstadt were many who, after the actual unveiling of the statue, would participate in a festive parade past the statue and past the grand-ducal birthday couple with its distinguished guests. The authorities had expected approximately 10,000 people to participate in this parade. An initial plan for the layout of Paradeplatz for the unveiling of the monument was published in *Darmstädter Zeitung* two weeks before the unveiling,[100] but had to be adjusted to accommodate the large number of participants and spectators. There was no space for the general public on the north side of Paradeplatz after all; these places were reserved for pupils of local schools and for certain sections of the military participating in the parade. Thus, space for the general public was cleared at the beginning of Rheinstrasse. The people standing there after the unveiling of the statue were expected to withdraw in an orderly manner to make room for the departure of the festive parade via Rheinstrasse.[101] *Darmstädter Zeitung* also published detailed information on exactly where and at what time the various groups of participants in the parade were to line up and what routes they had to take when marching in and out.[102] The parade, headed by the parade committee, comprised over a hundred groups in six sections, accompanied by regimental bands: 1) units of the garrison based in Darmstadt; 2) the presidium of warriors' association 'Hassia' with ca. 4,000 military men; 3) girls and women in colourful traditional costumes from Upper Hesse and delegations of the district administrations, the city and country communities, and chambers of commerce etc. of the Grand Duchy of Hesse; 4) student associations of the University of Giessen and the Technical College in Darmstadt; 5) groups of pupils of various

---

[100] *Darmstädter Zeitung*, 12 November 1898, afternoon edition.
[101] *Darmstädter Zeitung*, 22 November 1898, afternoon edition.
[102] *Darmstädter Zeitung*, 21 November 1898, afternoon edition.

schools in Darmstadt; and 6) groups of local associations and choral societies.[103]

The following detailed account of the festivities on 25 November was printed in the morning edition of *Darmstädter Zeitung* of Saturday 26 November 1898:[104]

Darmstadt, 25 November. The good relations between the ancestral Grand-ducal House of Hesse and by Rhine and the people of Hesse has found a new visible expression in the warmth and sympathy with which the whole of Hesse accepted the plan to erect a monument to its unforgettable Grand Duke Ludwig IV in Darmstadt, Hesse's capital, and in the eagerness with which people donated money and endeavoured to promote this beautiful undertaking. This work, stemming from mutual trust and love, was unveiled today, on the double birthday of the ruling grand-ducal couple, in the presence of all authoritative circles of the country, and was handed over to its intended purposes, to stand there in honourable memory for generations and generations and to serve as an ornament for the capital.

A lead grey November sky, which had sent down some rain during the night, lay over the city, as if the advanced season wished to assert itself without mercy. However, a welcome bright period in the forenoon continued beyond the noon hour, so the celebration was not marred. Yesterday evening, a tattoo ushered in the celebrations. It was followed today by a big reveille. Yesterday, the city was already bustling with life, and today it got busier and busier; trains – some of which had extra carriages – brought large crowds of people from all parts of the country into the city, which displayed rich decorations and flags, fir garlands,

---

[103] *Darmstädter Zeitung*, 21 November 1898, afternoon edition, and 26 November 1898, morning edition.

[104] 'Die Enthüllung des Reiterdenkmals', *Darmstädter Zeitung*, 26 November 1898, morning edition.

etc. in all parts of the city, particularly in Rheinstraße and on the monument square. In the morning, the festive day was heralded and choral music rang from the city tower. In addition, festive services were held in the Protestant town church, the Catholic parish church and the synagogue at the usual hour. Shortly after 10 am, the participants in the parade began lining up according to the given positions in the southern and western parts of the square. Numerous flags of corporations, the participating associations of the State University and the Technical College[105] in full dress, and particularly several hundred women and girls from Upper Hesse in their charming regional costumes created a colourful picture. The women and girls formed a line along the path of the grand-ducal couple and its high guests into the Residential Palace and scattered flowers on their path. The troops who participated in the celebration were commanded by Colonel Baron von Huene,[106] Commander of the 1st Grand-ducal Infantry (Life Guards) Regiment No. 115. These were, in particular: 1) a battalion of Infantry Regiment No. 115 comprising four combined companies with side arms, minstrels, and music; 2) one combined troop of each of the Dragoon Regiments Nos. 23 and 24; 3) two combined batteries of Field Artillery Regiment No. 25; 4) one combined battery of Train Battalion No. 25; 5) the Guards *Unteroffizier* company; 6) the flags of all regiments of the division, for each regiment accompanied by a *Feldwebel*, a *Sergeant*, an *Unteroffizier*, and two *Gefreiters*; 7) officers not listed here, as well as the medical officers and senior military officers of active rank, and a delegation of the non-active officers and doctors from the Darmstadt I and II *Landwehr* districts; 8) one deputation each from the officer corpses of the foreign regiments, including a regimental commander, a staff officer, a captain, and a lieutenant. The entire

---

[105] The University of Giessen and the Technical College in Darmstadt.
[106] Ernst Wilhelm, Baron von Hoiningen genannt Huene (1849–1924).

route from the New Palace to the Residential Palace was lined by troops.

In addition, the monument square and particularly the surroundings of the monument were beautifully prepared; the arrangements of the latter had obviously been guided by an artistic hand. The areas surrounding the monument, which itself stands on a granite substructure, were covered with fir branches to recreate an ambience of green lawns; in the wider area stood alternating single and double Venetian poles, effectively distinguished by flags, palms, and escutcheons displaying the coats of arms of towns in Hesse. Furthermore, the pavilion for the Grand Duke and Grand Duchess and their royal guests was erected in the south-west corner. The pavilion was mounted by a tastefully designed crown and was decorated with the most distinguished furniture, tapestries, etc. On the east side of the square, two mighty tribunes were erected, offering seats for the *Standesherren* (mediatized princes), the members of the ministries and subordinate authorities, the representatives of the clergy of the various confessions, the members of the *Ständekammern* (chambers of parliament), the representatives of the district administrations, and the city and country communities – accommodating approximately a thousand invitees.

The festively tuned crowd, numbering in the thousands, initially remained in exemplary order and calm. However, when Their Royal Highnesses the Grand Duke and Grand Duchess of Hesse, Her Royal Highness Princess Elisabeth of Hesse, His Royal Highness Prince Friedrich Leopold of Prussia, representing His Majesty the German Emperor, Her Grand-ducal Highness Princess Ludwig of Battenberg and the Princes Wilhelm and Heinrich of Hesse, Their Royal Highnesses the Duke and Princess Beatrice of Saxe-Coburg and Gotha, Their Imperial Highnesses Grand Duke and Grand Duchess Sergei of Russia, Their Serene Highnesses Prince and Princess Franz Joseph of Battenberg, and

Their Serene Highnesses Count and Countess Gustav of Erbach-Schönberg appeared on the monument square at 12 am, they were received by enthusiastic rallies, while the music corps intoned the anthem. After the first chairman of the monument committee, His Serene Highness Prince Bruno of Ysenburg and Büdingen, had asked the sovereign for permission to begin the unveiling ceremony, the ceremony was introduced in a consecratory manner by two stanzas of Friedrich Silcher's motet *'Herr Gott, Dich loben wir'* (Lord God, We Praise You), the final stanza of which was adapted to the celebration. The motet was performed by 25 local men's choruses, with approximately 670 members, under the direction of Mr Richard Senff.[107] Then, the secretary of the monument committee, president of the lower chamber, Reichstag member, *Geheimer Regierungsrat* Haas ascended the tribune to give the following ceremonial address:

Most Serene Grand Duke!

Most Serene Grand Duchess!

Thousands of loyal Hessians from all the regions of our beautiful homeland have gathered in Hesse's capital, Darmstadt, today as representatives of cities and villages, of authorities, corporations and public institutions who have been granted the privilege of celebrating a national festive event of a rare kind with Your Royal Highnesses, the Princes and Princesses of the Grand-ducal House and your royal relatives. Not only Your Royal Highness's most illustrious sisters who are unfortunately far away and other royal relatives, but also thousands and thousands of people in the country who are unable to attend are united with us in spirit in this solemn act of reverence and love.

A faithful people has undertaken to pay a debt of honour and gratitude to our much-loved Grand Duke Ludwig IV, a monarch who, according to God's mysterious plan, was recalled from this life in the prime and strength of his years.

---

[107] Richard Senff (1858–1932), a German composer, choir director and singing teacher.

Grand Duke Ludwig IV, who rests with God, has set himself a monument in the hearts of his contemporaries that is more valuable and everlasting than iron and stone. However, it is also important to inform future generations of the claim to recognition and gratitude of his country that the immortalised monarch has acquired through a government blessed with peace. In front of the castle of his ancestors, a monument has been erected to our deceased monarch, simple and plain in its decoration, but in keeping with the spirit of the immortalised person, which should be a shining sign for all time of how much the Hessian land was devoted to him in loyal, warm love, how much it appreciates his fatherly care and his services to the welfare of the people.

Soon after the news of the death of Grand Duke Ludwig IV had spread through the country, it became generally and quickly apparent that the tribute due to him had to be a genuine national affair. For this reason, the members of both chambers of the **Landstände** *[parliament] united with other outstanding men in an appeal to the entire population. Their appeal found a joyful echo in all parts of the country. Abundant gifts from high and low poured into the offering box, not the least of which came from thousands of hands of those less well-off. Thus, the basis for the realization of the project was soon laid.*

An excellent, highly gifted artist was selected to create a work to praise the late Grand Duke, bring honour to the country, and adorn the state capital. Efficient master builders and master workmen and industrious ordinary workmen put in their best to complete the work. Warm thanks are due to the artist, the masters, and workers, as well as to the patriotic men who effectively supported this beautiful enterprise.

And now the long-awaited moment has arrived, the moment when the monument dedicated to the memory of the immortalised grand duke shall be solemnly unveiled by his illustrious son, our most noble lord, and shall present itself in full splendour to the admiring eyes of those assembled. And this unveiling will take place in a meaningful connection with the celebration of the joint birthday of our illustrious grand-ducal couple, which is a day of joy and celebration for the whole of Hesse. But before the draping is pulled off, let us take a look into the past to let the richly blessed life of our immortalised monarch pass before our inner eyes. In our minds' eyes, we see the youthful prince at the side of his unforgettable wife, who was adorned with all virtues, but unfortunately was called away by God so early. We see him amidst his charming, blossoming children, where he set a noble example of intimate, glorious family life. We see the prince at the head of the Hessian troops, marching into the mighty war with the arch-enemy, where he was prepared to make sacrifices, selflessly and death-defyingly leading the way, enduring every hardship and danger like the least soldier, so as to return home as a gloriously crowned, victorious commander who was received with enthusiastic cries of jubilation. With heartfelt gratitude, we remember the blessings of his fifteen years of peaceful government. He carried out the duties of his lofty calling as a ruler with great dedication. Loyalty to the Emperor and the newly established empire, a free path for the development of the working population, the full guarantee of constitutional participation in the administration of the country for the people and their representatives, an open ear for everyone and fair consideration of their interests without regard to class, faith or party position – these were the foundations that, as brightly shining marks, gave the reign of Grand Duke Ludwig IV its distinctive character and made the prince popular in the true sense of the word. Mildness; justice; an open, honest, and chivalrous attitude; a rare kindness of heart; and a caring, fatherly affection for his country were the noble qualities by which he won all hearts and secured for himself a faithful and grateful memory for all time.

'Love for love, trust for trust, loyalty for loyalty' – this threefold motto was Ludwig IV's guide throughout his life and bound him closely to his people.

And when the draping will have been pulled off the statue and we recognize in it the dear friendly features of our monarch who rests with God, then all those loyal Hessians who are gathered here around our Grand-ducal House in this solemn hour – in memory of the noble deceased, and before the face of our reigning Grand Duke – want to unite anew on behalf of the entire Hessian people in the solemn pledge 'to stand by him and his House in good days and in bad days, in steadfast loyalty'!

That the coming generations may also remain faithful to this vow in the future, that the monument that is solemnly unveiled today may look down on our Grand-ducal House, protected and blessed by a benevolent destiny, and on a flourishing and happy Hesse for centuries to come! May God grant it!

Thereafter, the first chairman of the state monument committee, His Serene Highness the Prince of Ysenburg and Büdingen, requested His Royal Highness the Grand Duke to pull the draping off the statue. The Grand Duke did this amid loud cheering by the assembled crowd, who now saw before their eyes their beloved deceased Grand Duke, splendidly embodied in iron by an outstanding master's hand. At this solemn moment, bells began to ring. At the command of Colonel von Huene, the troops presented themselves while playing the presentation march, and a battery of Field Artillery Regiment No. 25 began a salute of 101 shots on the nearby Kleiner Exerzierplatz (small parade ground).[108]

Now, the first chairman of the state committee, His Serene Highness the Prince of Ysenburg and Büdingen, handed over the monument to the protection of the grand-ducal government, with the wish that the work may stand as a sign of true sentiment and gratitude for the deceased until the most distant times. The prince concluded his address with a threefold salute to Their Royal Highnesses the Grand Duke and the Grand Duchess. Then the bands enthusiastically broke into the anthem, *'Heil, unserm Fürsten Heil'* (Hail to our Grand Duke, hail!), which the crowd took up. Headed by the creator of the monument, Professor Friedrich

---

[108] Peter Engels, 'Exerzierplatz/Exert', Stadtlexikon Darmstadt (Historischer Verein für Hessen e. V.), accessed 28 January 2023.
https://www.darmstadt-stadtlexikon.de/e/exerzierplatz-/-exert.html.

Schaper from Berlin, the grand-ducal couple and their high guests then walked around the monument.

This was the end of the official ceremony.[109] The imposing procession of many thousands of participants began to move through the streets of the *'Neustadt'*, the [then] newer part of the city.[110] The procession included over a hundred groups, interspersed with regimental bands: the parade committee; the presidium of the warriors' association 'Hassia' with approximately four thousand military men and two music bands; girls and women in colourful traditional costumes from Upper Hesse; representatives of the district administrations, the city and country communities, and chambers of commerce etc. of the Grand Duchy of Hesse; the student bodies of the University of Giessen and the Technical College in Darmstadt; the Viktoria School and Girls' Institute; pupils from local primary and secondary schools, a craft school, and a construction school; several professional and voluntary fire brigades; the association 'Constantia' of Catholic businessmen; the Evangelical association of workers and craftsmen; over twenty-five choral societies; several military clubs, veterans' associations, an artillery association, and three privileged rifle clubs; the local athletes club 'Germania', about six gymnastics clubs, three fencing clubs, two cycling clubs, and a swimming club; three savings clubs; the

---

[109] Among the thousands of people who came to the unveiling, there were some who fainted. Unfortunately, the retired Major Bekker met a sadder fate. He suffered a stroke on the tribune and died shortly afterwards. He had participated as a member of the staff of then Prince Ludwig – subsequently Grand Duke Ludwig IV – in the first part of the campaign of 1870–1871 and fought in the Battle of Gravelotte and the Battle of Noisseville. (*Darmstädter Zeitung*, 26 November 1898, afternoon edition)

[110] Ekkehard Wiest, 'Mollerstadt', Stadtlexikon Darmstadt (Historischer Verein für Hessen e. V.), accessed 28 January 2023.
https://www.darmstadt-stadtlexikon.de/n/neue-vorstadt.html,
https://www.darmstadt-stadtlexikon.de/m/mollerstadt.html.

Bessungen citizens association;[111] a delegation of the city of Worms and its associations; the local catholic association of apprentices; the local catholic journeymen's association; the local butcher journeymen's association; the gardener's association, 'Feronia'; the local master roofers association; and more.

The wonderfully beautiful monument created by Professor Schaper, erected in humble proportions, distinguishes itself not in the least by excellent fidelity to the portrait of the man whom it glorifies – Grand Duke Ludwig IV. It was surrounded by a large crowd throughout the day, and generally received due appreciation. The plain granite pedestal is adorned only by a surrounding frieze of laurel leaves. Under the Hessian lion and crown on the front, it reads

Ludwig IV

and at the back

To the beloved and just prince
The brave leader of the Hessian troops 1870–1871
His loyal Hesse.

Grand Duke Ludwig IV appears in a simple tunic and field cap. The horse is a representation of a modern elegant riding horse with the graceful proportions characteristic of English horse-breeding. The steps and ramps are made of Zwingenberg[112] granite and the pedestal is made of Swedish granite, all made by the best workmanship. On the evening of 25 November, the monument shone in effective Bengal and electric floodlight illumination.

On the day of the unveiling, numerous laurel wreaths were laid at the monument by delegations of the state ministry, the city of Darmstadt, the local 'Melomanen' choral society, the Hessians living in Metz, etc. The wreath from the Hessians in Metz was laid

---

[111] Currently, Bessungen is a district of Darmstadt; however, in 1898, it was still an independent municipality south of Darmstadt.

[112] Zwingenberg is a village several kilometres south of Darmstadt.

by Captain Binnsack and made of foliage from the battlefield of the Bois de la Cusse.[104]

After the actual unveiling of the equestrian statue, a select group of high guests was invited to a gala banquet for 152 covers in the Kaiser Hall of the Grand-Ducal Residential Palace at half past two in the afternoon. During the banquet, His Royal Highness the Grand Duke raised a toast to his loyal people of Hesse, while Prince Bruno of Ysenburg and Büdingen toasted Their Royal Highnesses the Grand Duke and the Grand Duchess.[113]

Meanwhile, to celebrate the unveiling of the monument dedicated to Grand Duke Ludwig IV and the birth anniversaries of Grand Duke Ernst Ludwig and Grand Duchess Victoria Melita, a large number of participants from all over the Grand Duchy gathered at 2 pm on 25 November for a banquet in the large hall of the 'Saalbau'. The civil servants and citizens of the capital were well represented, and a number of inactive officers were also present. The hall was festively decorated for the occasion, with greenery and draperies in the Hessian and Saxe-Coburg national colours. On the podium, the busts of His Royal Highness Grand Duke Ernst Ludwig and His Royal Highness Grand Duke Ludwig IV were displayed. During the meal, *Beigeordneter* Karl Schliephake raised a toast. It was received with great enthusiasm and those gathered joyfully joined in the three cheers. The toast was followed by the national anthem, which was performed by the band of Grand-ducal Field Artillery Regiment No. 25 (Grand-ducal Artillery Corps).[114]

For high guests, the day ended with a splendid evening programme in the Grand Ducal theatre in Darmstadt. It was attended by, among others, Grand Duke Ernst Ludwig and Grand Duchess Victoria Melita of Hesse and by Rhine, Grand Duke

---

[113] *Darmstädter Zeitung*, 26 November 1898, afternoon edition.
[114] *Darmstädter Zeitung*, 26 November 1898, afternoon edition.

Sergei Alexandrovich and Grand Duchess Elisabeth of Russia, the Duke of Saxe-Coburg and Gotha, Princess Beatrice of Saxe-Coburg and Gotha, Princess Victoria of Battenberg, Prince Albert of Schleswig-Holstein, Prince Heinrich and Prince Wilhelm of Hesse, Count and Countess Gustav of Erbach-Schönberg, and Prince Franz Joseph of Battenberg and his wife Princess Anna. The programme began with a speech by Adolf Morneweg (1851–1909), the Mayor of Darmstadt. He ended with three cheers, after which the court orchestra played the national anthem. Then, the curtain rose and revealed the crowned bust of His Royal Highness Grand Duke Ludwig IV in a portico, standing out from a green palm and laurel grove. With great warmth and proven art of declamation, court actress Frieda Eichelsheim (1873–1953) – in the guise of Darmstadt's patroness Hassia – delivered a poetic prologue written by Baron Karl Schenk zu Schweinsberg-Wäldershausen that celebrated the importance of the festive day. It ended with a toast to Their Royal Highnesses the Grand Duke and Grand Duchess, whereupon the audience sang the anthem *'Heil, unserm Fürsten Heil'* standing. This homage was followed by a performance of Richard Wagner's opera entitled *'Das Rheingold'* (The Rhinegold), led by court music director Willem de Haan (1849–1930).[115]

Several cities and villages in Hesse wanted to contribute to the festivities in connection with the unveiling of the equestrian statue in their own way. For example, Offenbach, Seligenstadt, Gundheim, and Grünberg put up decorations and festive lights in the streets.[116] In the city of Mainz, a festive performance took place in the local theatre on 25 November.[117] The number of people from the town of Bad Nauheim who participated in the festivities in Darmstadt was so large that the usual local festive dinner on the

---

[115] *Darmstädter Zeitung*, 26 November 1898, afternoon edition.
[116] *Darmstädter Zeitung*, 26 November 1898, afternoon edition.
[117] *Darmstädter Zeitung*, 28 November 1898, afternoon edition.

occasion of the Grand Duke's and Grand Duchess's birthday in Hotel 'Kursaal' had to be postponed for one day to 26 November. This gave the mayor of Bad Nauheim, who had attended the unveiling, the opportunity to provide a detailed account of the festivities in Darmstadt the day before.[118]

In addition, parties were also organized for specific groups. One group that certainly deserved a festive evening was that of the workers who had been involved in the production and installation of the equestrian statue. A feast was hosted for them at the 'Zur Krone' brewery tavern. Prince Bruno of Ysenburg and Büdingen, president of the upper chamber, and *Geheimer Regierungsrat* Haas, president of the lower chamber, gave speeches and thanked the workers for their excellent work.[119] Hotel 'Zur Traube' hosted a festive dinner for retired officers, where General of the Cavalry Wilhelm von Winterfeldt (1824–1906) made a speech. On the evening of 25 November, the Technical College of Darmstadt organised a festive evening, which included a talk on methods and tasks of general economics in its great hall.[120]

And then there were the students. The student corps of the State University of Giessen, where Ludwig IV and his brother Heinrich had studied, organised a commercium in a banquet hall in Giessen on the evening of 25 November; former students were also welcome to this event.[121] The Giessen Wingolf student fraternity organised a commercium in Restaurant 'Zur Stadt Pfungstadt' in Darmstadt, also on 25 November.[122] In addition, the

---

[118] *Darmstädter Zeitung*, 28 November 1898, afternoon edition.
[119] *Darmstädter Zeitung*, 26 November 1898, afternoon edition. See also Mona Sauer and Peter Engels, 'Krone', Stadtlexikon Darmstadt (Historischer Verein für Hessen e. V.), accessed 28 January 2023, https://www.darmstadt-stadtlexikon.de/k/krone.html.
[120] *Darmstädter Zeitung*, 26 November 1898, afternoon edition.
[121] *Darmstädter Zeitung*, 18 November 1898, morning edition.
[122] *Darmstädter Zeitung*, 23 November 1898, morning edition. See also Peter Engels, 'Sitte', Stadtlexikon Darmstadt (Historischer Verein für Hessen e. V.),

ADC *Burschenschaft* (a certain type of student association) held its commercium in Hotel 'Zur Traube' in Darmstadt.[123]

The girls and women in traditional costumes from Upper Hesse who had participated in the festive parade had contributed to the festive nature of the unveiling in colourful ways. Grand Duchess Victoria Melita received a delegation of them in the New Palace in Darmstadt on Saturday 26 November. At the end of the afternoon of that day, an extra train ran to Upper Hesse to bring these girls and women and other people who had attended the festivities back home. They were waved goodbye to by the people they had stayed with. It was a heartfelt goodbye.[124]

The royal guests also went their way. *Darmstädter Zeitung* tells us that Prince Friedrich Leopold of Prussia already left Darmstadt shortly after 4 pm on 25 November.[125] The Duke of Saxe-Coburg and Gotha left Darmstadt for Coburg in the morning of Monday 28 November, while Grand Duke Sergei and Grand Duchess Elisabeth returned to Moscow later that week.[126]

---

accessed 28 January 2023,
https://www.darmstadt-stadtlexikon.de/s/sitte.html.
[123] *Darmstädter Zeitung*, 28 November 1898, afternoon edition.
[124] *Darmstädter Zeitung*, 28 November 1898, afternoon edition.
[125] *Darmstädter Zeitung*, 26 November 1898, afternoon edition.
[126] *Darmstädter Zeitung*, 28 November 1998, afternoon edition.

Conclusion

When the equestrian statue of Grand Duke Ludwig IV was unveiled on 25 November 1898, Paradeplatz in Darmstadt already had another monument – a war monument for the miliary men fallen in the 1870–1871 Franco-German war. It was designed by the German sculptor August Herzig (1846–1919) and was erected and unveiled in front of the *Exerzierhaus* (drill house) in 1879, which stood on the site of what is currently the *Hessisches Landesmuseum*.[127] This monument was damaged in 1945 and taken down in 1952.[128]

The equestrian statue in Darmstadt was not the only monument dedicated to Grand Duke Ludwig IV in Hesse either. Two more monuments were erected to honour Grand Duke Ludwig IV in the Grand Duchy of Hesse, one in the city of Worms and one in the town of Bingen am Rhein, both in the province of Rhineland of the Grand Duchy of Hesse and by Rhine. The local government of Worms erected an obelisk for Grand Duke Ludwig IV on its local Paradeplatz, today's Ludwigsplatz, with financial contributions from the city's inhabitants. It was unveiled by Grand Duke Ernst Ludwig and Grand Duchess Victoria Melita of Hesse in 1895. Initially, the monument commemorated the military achievements of the Grand Duke as commander of the Grand-ducal Hessian troops in the Franco-Prussian War of 1870–1871. However, the square and monument underwent several changes over the years, and the inscription now praises Ludwig IV as a promoter of trade, industry and the arts. Years later, in 1913,

---

[127] Mona Sauer, 'Exerzierhaus', Stadtlexikon Darmstadt (Historischer Verein für Hessen e. V.), accessed 6 January 2023.
https://www.darmstadt-stadtlexikon.de/e/exerzierhaus.html.

[128] Friedrich Wilhelm Kniess, 'Kriegerdenkmäler', Stadtlexikon Darmstadt (Historischer Verein für Hessen e. V.), accessed 6 January 2023.
https://www.darmstadt-stadtlexikon.de/k/kriegerdenkmaeler.html.

the town of Bingen am Rhein in Rhineland got a large bronze statue of Ludwig IV, funded by the local *Kommerzienrat* (Councillor of Commerce) Julius Woog. The statue sits in Hindenburganlage park, next to what was then the *Festhalle*, a banqueting hall.

The equestrian statue of Grand Duke Ludwig IV in Darmstadt initially stood in the middle of Paradeplatz. However, the statue was temporarily removed for the construction of an underground car park under the square in 1967. It was placed back subsequently, without steps and ramps, at the south-eastern corner of the square.[129] In 1949, shortly after World War II, the square where Grand Ludwig IV's equestrian statue stands was renamed Friedensplatz – Peace Square.

---

[129] Mona Sauer, 'Reiterdenkmal', Stadtlexikon Darmstadt (Historischer Verein für Hessen e. V.), accessed 6 January 2023.
https://www.darmstadt-stadtlexikon.de/r/reiterdenkmal.html.

Bibliography

Alice Grand Duchess of Hesse. *Alice, Grand Duchess of Hesse, Princess of Great Britain and Ireland: Biographical Sketch and Letters*. New York: G. P. Putnam's Sons, 1885.

Baur, Fidel von. *Die Operationen des achten Deutschen Bundes-Corps im Feldzuge des Jahres 1866: Nach authentischen Quellen dargestellt*. Darmstadt: Zernin, 1868.

Bender, Ferdinand. *Elisabeth, Prinzessin Carl von Hessen und bei Rhein, geb. Prinzessin von Preussen: Ein Lebensbild*. Darmstadt: Waitz, 1886.

Buxhoeveden, Sophie. *The Life and Tragedy of Alexandra Feodorovna, Empress of Russia: A Biography*. London: Longmans, Green, 1930.

Die Hessen in der Schlacht bei Gravelotte-St. Privat, ein Gedenkblatt zur Enthüllungsfeier des Landes-Krieger-Denkmals am 18. August 1879. Darmstadt: Zernin, 1879.

Erbach-Schönberg, Marie Fürstin zu. *Memoiren 1852–1923*. Geschichtsblätter Kreis Bergstrasse. Sonderband 13. Lorsch: Verlag Laurissa, 1991.

Ernst Ludwig Grossherzog von Hessen und bei Rhein, Eckhart G. Franz, and Golo Mann. *Erinnertes: Aufzeichnungen des letzten Grossherzogs Ernst Ludwig von Hessen und bei Rhein*. Darmstadt: E. Roether, 1983.

Hoenig, Fritz August. *Der Volkskrieg an der Loire im Herbst 1870; Nach amtlichen Quellen und handschriftlichen Aufzeichnungen von Mitkämpfern* (Vol. 5). Berlin: Mittler, 1897.

Hough, Richard. *Louis & Victoria: The Family History of the Mountbattens*. 2nd ed. London: Weidenfeld and Nicolson, 1984.

In Luft und Sonne: Künstler- und Selbstschriften-Album; Im Einverständnis mit der Zentralstelle der Deutschen Vereinigungen für Ferienkolonien und Sommerpflegen. Berlin: Schorers Familienblatt, 1888.

Kleinpenning, Petra H. *The Correspondence of the Empress Alexandra of Russia with Ernst Ludwig and Eleonore, Grand Duke and Duchess of Hesse 1878-1916.* Norderstedt: BoD – Books on Demand, 2010.

Knodt, Manfred. *Ernst Ludwig Grossherzog von Hessen und bei Rhein: Sein Leben und Seine Zeit.* 2nd ed. Darmstadt: Schlapp, 1985.

Martin, Theodore. *The Life of His Royal Highness The Prince Consort* (Vol. V). New York: Appleton & Co., 1880.

Milford Haven, Victoria Marchioness of. *Recollections: The Memoirs of Victoria Marchioness of Milford Haven, 1863–1914.* Typescript of the recollections. Broadlands archives. MS62/MB/21. University of Southampton Special Collections. Southampton, UK, n.d. https://cdn.southampton.ac.uk/assets/imported/transforms/content-block/UsefulDownloads_Download/F419AA816BFC4674981B7BEA9538BD33/MB21_transcript.pdf.

Nicholas II. *Dnevniki Imperatora Nikolaja II (1894–1918): 1894–1904.* Edited by Sergei Vladimirovich Mironenko. Moscow: Rosspen, 2011.

Nicholas II. *The Diaries of Nicholas II: 1897–1900.* Translated, edited and annotated by Stephen R. de Angelis. USA: Bookemon, 2014.

Noel, Gerard. *Princess Alice: Queen Victoria's Forgotten Daughter.* London: Constable, 1974.

Scherf, H., and A. Draudt. *Die Theilnahme der Grossherzöglichen Hessischen (25.) Division an dem Feldzug 1870-1871 gegen Frankreich*. 2 Volumes. Darmstadt: Buchhandlung Großherzoglichen Staatsverlags, 1877/1883.

Tsekhanovetskiy, Vladislav Pavlovitch. *Istoriya 18 Dragunskogo Klyastitskogo ego korolevskogo vysotchestva velikogo gertsoga Gessenskogo polka: 1806–1886*. Warsaw: Tipografiya brat'ev Ezhinskikh, 1886. https://runivers.ru/bookreader/book58461/#page/1/mode/1up.

Victoria, Queen of the United Kingdom, and Arthur Helps. *Leaves from the Journal of Our Life in the Highlands: From 1848 to 1861; Earlier Visits to Scotland, and Tours in England and Ireland and Yachting Excursions*. London: Smith, Elder, 1868.

Victoria, Queen of the United Kingdom, and Richard Hough. *Advice to a Grand-Daughter: Letters from Queen Victoria to Princess Victoria of Hesse*. London: Heinemann, 1975.

Zernin, Eduard. *Ein Lebensbild von Ludwig IV., Grossherzog von Hessen und bei Rhein. Festschrift zur Feier der Enthüllung des Reiterdenkmals zu Darmstadt. Mit allerhöchster Erlaubnis Seiner Königlichen Hoheit des Grossherzogs Ernst Ludwig*. Darmstadt: Grossherzoglicher Staatsverlag, 1898.

Zimmermann, Karl von. *Der Antheil der Grossherzoglich Hessischen Armee-Division am Kriege 1866*. Kriegsgeschichtliche Einzelschriften. Heft 22 and Heft 23. Berlin: E.S. Mittler und Sohn, 1897.

Newspapers

Darmstädter Zeitung

Hessisches Regierungsblatt

Websites

Engels, Peter. 'Exerzierplatz/Exert'. Stadtlexikon Darmstadt (Historischer Verein für Hessen e. V.). Accessed 28 January 2023. https://www.darmstadt-stadtlexikon.de/e/exerzierplatz-/-exert.html.

Engels, Peter. 'Sitte'. Stadtlexikon Darmstadt (Historischer Verein für Hessen e. V.). Accessed 28 January 2023. https://www.darmstadt-stadtlexikon.de/s/sitte.html.

Kniess, Friedrich Wilhelm. 'Kriegerdenkmäler'. Stadtlexikon Darmstadt. Historischer Verein für Hessen e. V. Accessed 6 January 2023. https://www.darmstadt-stadtlexikon.de/k/kriegerdenkmaeler.html.

Sauer, Mona, and Peter Engels. 'Krone'. Stadtlexikon Darmstadt. Historischer Verein für Hessen e. V. Accessed 28 January 2023. https://www.darmstadt-stadtlexikon.de/k/krone.html.

Sauer, Mona. 'Reiterdenkmal'. Stadtlexikon Darmstadt. Historischer Verein für Hessen e. V. Accessed 6 January 2023. https://www.darmstadt-stadtlexikon.de/r/reiterdenkmal.html.

Wiest, Ekkehard. 'Mollerstadt'. Stadtlexikon Darmstadt. Historischer Verein für Hessen e. V. Accessed 28 January 2023. https://www.darmstadt-stadtlexikon.de/m/mollerstadt.html.

Index

Albert, Prince of Saxe-Coburg and Gotha, Prince Consort of Queen Victoria, 43, 44
Albert, Prince of Schleswig-Holstein, 93
Albrecht, Prince of Prussia, 61
Alexander II, Tsar of Russia, 33
Alexander, Prince of Battenberg, 35
Alexander, Prince of Hesse and by Rhine, 35, 36
Alexandra. *See* Alix, Princess of Hesse and by Rhine, Empress Alexandra Empress Alexandra Feodorovna of Russia of Russia
Alfred, Duke of Saxe-Coburg and Gotha, 80, 85, 93, 95
Alice, Princess of the United Kingdom, Grand Duchess of Hesse and by Rhine, 13, 16, 21, 35, 42, 43, 44, 45, 46, 49, 55, 58, 59
Alix, Princess of Hesse and by Rhine, Empress Alexandra Feodorovna of Russia, 14, 61, 63, 78, 79
Anna, Princess of Hesse and by Rhine, 23
Anna, Princess of Montenegro, Princess of Battenberg, 85, 93
Beatrice, Princess of Saxe-Coburg and Gotha, 85, 93
Becker, Theodor Andreas, 23, 28
Bekker, Major, 90
Bender, Ferdinand, 22, 23, 25
Berg, Baron von, 41
Bernard, Hereditary Duke of Saxe-Meiningen, 59

Bismarck-Schönhausen, Otto von, 35, 48
Buxhoeveden, Sophie, 14, 63
Carl, Prince of Hesse and by Rhine, 20, 22, 25, 31, 32, 33, 57
Charlotte, Princess of Prussia, 58, 59
Curtius, Ernst, 27, 28, 30, 31
Eichelsheim, Frieda, 93
Eigenbrodt, Karl, 64
Elisabeth Anne, Princess of Prussia, 59
Elisabeth, Princess of Hesse and by Rhine, 85
Elisabeth, Princess of Hesse and by Rhine, Grand Duchess Elizaveta Feodorovna of Russia, 28, 78, 85, 93, 95
Elisabeth, Princess of Prussia, Princess of Hesse and by Rhine, 20, 21, 22, 23, 35, 36, 38, 39
Emil, Prince of Hesse and by Rhine, 25, 49, 70
Erbach-Schönberg, Count Gustav of, 86, 93
Erbach-Schönberg, Countess Marie of, 86, 93
Ernst Ludwig, Grand Duke of Hesse and by Rhine, 13, 14, 32, 34, 47, 54, 63, 68, 77, 79, 85, 92, 96
Ernst, 4th Prince of Leiningen, 64
Feder, Karl August, 23
Fischer, Friedrich Leopold, 26, 27
Franz Joseph, Emperor of Austria, 58
Franz Joseph, Prince of Battenberg, 85, 93

Friedrich August, Hereditary Grand Duke of Oldenburg, 59
Friedrich III, King of Prussia, German Emperor, 26, 27, 28, 31, 33, 60
Friedrich Karl, Prince of Prussia, 68
Friedrich Leopold, Prince of Prussia, 80, 85, 95
Friedrich Wilhelm III, King of Prussia, 20
Friedrich Wilhelm IV, King of Prussia, 22, 33, 37
Georg, Prince of Hesse and by Rhine, 25
German, Daniel, 67
Gladenbeck, Paul, 77
Gladenbeck, Walter, 77
Grolman, Adolf von, 23, 26, 31
Haan, Willem de, 93
Haas, Wilhelm, 77, 78, 86, 94
Hahn, fencing master, 24
Hansen, Professor, 29, 30, 31
Hauke, Countess Julia, Princess of Battenberg, 35
Heijl, Major von, 80
Heinrich, Prince of Hesse and by Rhine, 20, 21, 23, 25, 26, 28, 31, 32, 35, 36, 38, 39, 42, 44, 70, 80, 85, 93, 94
Heinrich, Prince of Prussia, 60, 61, 78
Heldenberg, Miss von, 24
Helene, Duchess of Orléans, 21
Herbold, Anton Friedrich, 24
Herzig, August, 96
Hessert, Ferdinand von, 70
Hoenig, Fritz, 67, 69
Huene, Ernst Wilhelm von, 84, 89
Irene, Princess of Hesse and by Rhine, Princess Heinrich of Prussia, 60, 61, 78, 79

Jäger, Wilhelm, 64
Kattrein, Captain, 50, 51
Kessel, Major von, 41
Kussmaul, Adolf, 64
Lautenberger, Major, 51
Löbell, Professor, 27, 28
Louis Philippe I, King of France, 21
Louise, Queen Consort of Denmark, 79
Lucas, August, 24
Ludwig I, Grand Duke of Hesse and by Rhine, 70
Ludwig II, Grand Duke of Hesse and by Rhine, 20
Ludwig II, King of Bavaria, 57
Ludwig III, Grand Duke of Hesse and by Rhine, 20, 22, 25, 26, 32, 33, 35, 36, 37, 38, 45, 46, 53, 55, 57, 58
Ludwig IV, Grand Duke of Hesse and by Rhine, 13, passim
Ludwig, Landgrave of Hesse-Homburg, 20
Ludwig, Prince of Battenberg, 35, 78
Mangold, Carl Amadeus, 25
Maria Anna, Princess of Prussia, 20
Maria Nikolaevna, Grand Duchess of Russia, 80
Marie, Princess of Hesse and by Rhine, 59
Marie, Princess of Prussia, Queen of Bavaria, 23
Mathilde, Princess of Bavaria, Grand Duchess of Hesse and by Rhine, 22, 36, 44
Maximilian II, King of Bavaria, 23
Monnard, Professor, 27, 28
Morneweg, Adolf, 93
Müller, Heinrich, 77, 78
Nakhimov, Pavel Stepanovich, 79

Napoleon II, Emperor of the French, 48
Nicholas II, Emperor of Russia, 79
Nordeck zur Rabenau, Friedrich von, 33
Perthes, Professor, 28, 30
Schäffer-Bernstein, Friedrich Ferdinand von, 25, 38, 39
Schaper, Friedrich, 19, 77, 90, 91
Schenk zu Schweinsberg-Wäldershausen, Karl, 93
Schliephake, Karl, 92
Schlitz gen. von Görtz, Carl, 41
Senff, Richard, 86
Sergei Alexandrovich, Grand Duke of Russia, 28, 78, 85, 93, 95
Silcher, Friedrich, 86
Sligo, Mrs J., 56
Spiess, Adolf, 24
Spiess, Edmund, 24
Thomas, Heinrich Ludwig, 24
Victoria Melita, Princess of Saxe-Coburg and Gotha, Grand Duchess of Hesse and by Rhine, 14, 77, 85, 92, 95, 96
Victoria, Princess of Hesse and by Rhine, Princess Ludwig of Battenberg, Marchioness of Milford Haven, 14, 35, 63, 78, 85, 93

Victoria, Princess of Saxe-Coburg-Saalfeld, Duchess of Kent, 43
Victoria, Queen of the United Kingdom of Great Britain and Ireland, 13, 16, 42, 43, 45, 46, 54, 63
Victoria, the Princess Royal, 26
Wagner, Richard, 93
Waitz, Professor, 30, 31
Walter, Professor, 27, 28, 30
Wernher, Paul, 78
Westerweller von Anthoni, Paul, 78
Wiegand, Mr, 24
Wilhelm I, King of Prussia, German Emperor, 22, 37, 39, 40, 44, 54, 55, 56, 59
Wilhelm II, German Emperor, 59, 60, 61, 62, 63, 80
Wilhelm, Prince of Hesse and by Rhine, 23, 85, 93
Wilhelm, Prince of Prussia, 20, 35
Willich gen. von Pöllnitz, Caroline, 21
Winterfeldt, Wilhelm von, 94
Wittich, Major General von, 48
Woog, Julius, 97
Wrangel, Karl von, 47
Ysenburg and Büdingen, Bruno Prince of, 14, 77, 86, 89, 92, 94
Zernin, Gebhard, 14, 15, 16, 17, 18, 19, 78